More than Land or Sky

Art from Appalachia

More than Land or Sky

Art from Appalachia

Barbara Shissler Nosanow

Published for the National Museum of American Art
by the Smithsonian Institution Press
Washington, D.C., 1981

Published on the occasion of an exhibition organized by the National Museum of American Art, Smithsonian Institution, Washington, D.C., and shown there October 30, 1981–January 3, 1982, before traveling to museums throughout the thirteen-state Appalachian region.

Curator for the Exhibition:
Barbara Shissler Nosanow,
Curator for Education, NMAA

Installation Design:
Christopher C. Addison, NMAA

Editor in Chief, NMAA:
Carroll S. Clark

Publication Designer, SI Press:
Polly Sexton

Cover:
Victor Huggins, *Near Salem*, 1975,
cat. no. 44.

Library of Congress Cataloging in Publication Data

Nosanow, Barbara Shissler.
    More than land or sky.

    "Published on the occasion of an exhibition organized by the National Museum of American Art, Smithsonian Institution, Washington, D.C., and shown there October 30, 1981–January 3, 1982, before traveling to museums throughout the thirteen-state Appalachian region"—T.p. verso.
    1. Art,   American—Appalachian region—Exhibitions. I. National Museum of American Art (U.S.) II. Title.
N6516.N67   709'.74'074014   81-13566

                            AACR2

Photographic Credits

American Folklife Center, Library of Congress, cat. no. 30
Lisa Berg, cat. no. 21
Brunner Studio, fig. 3; cat. nos. 18, 62
Geoffrey Clements, cat. no. 93
Bevan Davies, cat. no. 76
Cameron Dennis, cat. nos. 40, 60
E. W. George, fig. 13; cat. nos. 69, 70, 71, 72, 73
Larry Hopewell, cat. no. 74
Don Lehman, cat. nos. 64, 65, 66
John Lloyd Photography, cat. no. 55
Jerry Martin, cat. no. 5
David Matthews, fig. 12
Pat Mills, cat. nos. 19, 20
Steve Payne, fig. 9; cat. nos. 7, 81, 88, 101, 102
Jon Reis, fig. 19; cat. nos. 3, 4
Roanoke Museum of Fine Arts, cover
Margo N. Rosenbaum, cat. nos. 85, 86
Walter Rosenblum, cat. no. 10
Steve Skrzypek, fig. 11; cat. no. 37
Richard A. Stoner, cat. no. 16
Rick Webb Studio, cat. nos. 79, 80

Contents

Honorary Sponsoring Committee

Alabama, The Honorable Fob James, Governor
Georgia, The Honorable George Busbee, Governor
Kentucky, The Honorable John Y. Brown, Jr., Governor
Maryland, The Honorable Harry Hughes, Governor
Mississippi, The Honorable William F. Winter, Governor
New York, The Honorable Hugh L. Carey, Governor
North Carolina, The Honorable James B. Hunt, Jr., Governor
Ohio, The Honorable James A. Rhodes, Governor
Pennsylvania, The Honorable Dick Thornburgh, Governor
South Carolina, The Honorable Richard W. Riley, Governor
Tennessee, The Honorable Lamar Alexander, Governor
Virginia, The Honorable John N. Dalton, Governor
West Virginia, The Honorable John D. Rockefeller IV, Governor

Statement

The possibility of an exhibition of art from Appalachia was first raised more than two years ago by Ann Bray, then of the Appalachian Regional Commission, in a conversation with Joshua C. Taylor, director of the National Museum of American Art (NMAA) from 1970 until his death in April 1981. Ann Bray, a native Appalachian from Harlan, Kentucky, suggested that such an idea might be worth investigating, but Taylor was wary. Quality was always his primary concern, and beyond questions of excellence were also those of definition and theme, necessary prerequisites before any exhibition was undertaken at the NMAA under his direction. Yet, the idea of the way in which the place where an artist lives may affect his work was one that interested Taylor and stirred his imagination. Moreover, he was always interested in seeing stereotypical images debunked, and Appalachian art to most people suggested time-honored crafts practiced in traditional ways by backwoods craftsmen. Taylor therefore suggested that an investigation of the fine arts of the region might be in order, that the theme of the proposed exhibition might be an examination of the influence of place upon the work of contemporary Appalachian artists, and that a small selection of works by these artists might be undertaken for presentation at NMAA provided he could be convinced that their work was of sufficient quality to merit exhibition. Barbara Shissler Nosanow of the NMAA was designated curator for the exhibition, and with deputy curator Margaret P. Cogswell thereupon began thousands of miles of travel from New York State down the chain of mountains that marks Appalachia to the northern counties of Mississippi and Alabama. Taylor, meanwhile, waited to be convinced.

The size of the exhibition now assembled—105 works by 69 artists—attests to the excellence of the work that the curators viewed. Persuaded by their findings, Taylor decided to enlarge the exhibition from the small showing originally envisioned to NMAA's major exhibition for fall 1981. Funded in part by a generous grant from the Appalachian Regional Commission, the exhibition will tour throughout the thirteen-state Appalachian region after closing at the NMAA. While on view here it will be accompanied by a number of exhibition-related programs—films, workshops, concerts, poetry readings, and seminars. These will help place the works on view within their cultural context and will make a broad and diverse range of Appalachian arts available to the Washington public. It is our hope that similar programs can be planned to accompany the exhibition as it tours. Nothing would have pleased Joshua Taylor more. Always noted for his broad and unconventional taste, he was also a master teacher whose approach stressed the delights of individual discovery, the pleasures of perceiving unexpected interrelationships within the web of American art and culture. It is our belief that the fine arts of Appalachia will surprise the American public, not only by their excellence but by their individuality, range, and diversity, and that the exhibition will be of national interest.

Our thanks for help with this endeavor thus go, first of all, to Ann Bray, whose vision first sparked our interest in the fine arts of this area and whose persistent belief in the validity of the concept helped make the exhibition possible; to the Appalachian Regional Commission for the generous grant that provided major funding for this undertaking; and to the governors of the thirteen Appalachian states, who have acted as honorary sponsors of the show. Their continued sponsorship during the tour of the exhibition will help insure its success as it travels. We also wish to acknowledge the initial interest and support of Richard Murray, former curator of education at NMAA and now director of the Birmingham Museum of Art, Alabama, to whom representatives of the ARC first mentioned the possibility of this project.

Barbara Shissler Nosanow, as curator for the exhibition, has planned the programs associated with it. She has been ably assisted here and in her travel by her deputy, Margaret Cogswell, and by Anne Timpano and Nancy R. Adelson, who have acted as research assistants for the project, and who, among other duties, provided biographical information on each artist and documentary data for each work included in the catalogue. Claudia T. Esko, a graduate intern at NMAA from Pennsylvania State University, has been their assistant and with them has also provided catalogue text. Audrey L. Fuller, Colleen W. Brown, and Marjorie M. Tuttle have given the dedicated secretarial support without which no project comes to fruition.

We hope that the exhibition will convince all visitors that Appalachian art is indeed more than the surface treatment of the beauty of land and sky. Its lyric power and quirky individuality are deeply rooted in the traditions of the region and in the traditions of American art in general. We hope, further, that it will prove as stimulating to visitors as it did to the man to whose memory we dedicate our exhibition—our late director, Joshua C. Taylor.

Harry Lowe
Acting Director
National Museum of American Art

I've got more than this old world can ever hold,
I've got more than all the silver and all the gold,
I've got more than land or sky,
I've got more than all the money in this old world
   could ever buy.

I've got more than land or sea,
Let it be, oh Lord, let it be.

from "This Old World," an original song
by Howard Finster. Reprinted by permission.

The Appalachian Region

More than Land or Sky: Art from Appalachia

Appalachia: land of mists and reverie, of myths, visions, and stories; land of ephemeral, softly vibrating light; of contrasts—panoramic views of sweep and power alternating with sensuous, gentle curves of mountain slopes, vistas contrasting with glades and thickets rich in leaf and flower. Yet, a land and people hard and resilient, formed in adversity, for long years isolated from the mainstream of contemporary life, deeply rooted in custom and in their own sharply defined way of life; a people at once naïve and canny, independent, fiercely individual, suspicious, proud. In what way is their artistic vision affected by the place in which they live? What is its character? Does it reflect their roots, their traditions? Is there indeed in the fine arts of these people a specific sense of place that may emerge beyond the stereotypes of "down-home" crafts perpetuated in time-honored forms?

These were the questions that preoccupied us as we began our thousands of miles of travel throughout the thirteen-state Appalachian region in preparation for the present exhibition. With the exception of some of the "folk artists" who have emerged and whom we proudly include in the exhibition along with their visually more broadly educated peers, the men and women represented are not cut off from contemporary American life or uninformed about current work or art circles in New York, Washington, Chicago, or even California. Many have studied at prestigious art schools, primarily in the Midwest and on the East Coast. Yet all have chosen to remain in, or return to, Appalachia—or in the case of some (Steven A. Barbash and Angelo Ippolito, for example) to adopt Appalachia as their home; its sights, textures, light, and spatial configurations as the context and substance of their art. Lowell Hayes's eloquent statement informs us of a spiritual journey made, in effect, by many of the artists in the exhibition, a voyage to contemporary, urban America, and, then, the return home again:

> (The opening shot of World War II) blew away a whole culture right here in my own hills, in my own lifetime. Consequently, much of my growing up . . . was occupied with acculturation. Like an immigrant I had to be naturalized in order to find a place in the new culture, with the difference that I did not immigrate; the new culture, rather, came to my homeland. . . . My parents prospered as enthusiastic participants in this exciting new (to them) culture of Progress. . . . I was the first from either side of my family to go to college. I traveled, went to seminary (Divinity School of the University of Chicago), gorged myself to the point of overindulgence at the world's cultural banquet. I was a social activist, an antiarchitect, a schoolteacher, a minister, a creator of institutions, a corporation president. Like any other hillbilly who comes home, I realized eventually that what I really wanted was what I could find at home. . . . Out of what I find here I make expressions of what I find here.

What have these artists made? How can we characterize their work? What has emerged is an art of diversity and of strength of character, one united not so much by style or formal configurations as by a common sentiment, feeling, and—to use an old-fashioned word—content. Wishing to live where they feel at home both physically and spiritually, the artists of Appalachia have developed an approach to art that is nondoctrinaire. Consistent with the present pluralism in the arts, a period some critics have referred to as "postmodernist," their approach is broadly tolerant and inclusive. These artists feel no incentive to be determinedly modern, to fight the battle for the avant-garde, shocking friends and neighbors as last-ditch defenders of the right of art to be incomprehensibly new. The reductive, nonobjective styles of the recent past have been, if not rejected by them, then overlooked or ignored. Thus, although their work is not specifically antimodernist, it is different—and as such must be judged by different standards. Although largely figurative, their art is not for this reason reactionary or retrograde, nor is it any sentimental attempt to escape into an imagined past. In creating his remarkable room hanging (fig. 1) in this exhibition, Lowell Hayes rummages, like his quilt-making grandmother before him, through bags of scraps or material collected helter-skelter from every imaginable source. He is foraging to create something individual, something uniquely his own. Just so, other artists of this geographic area pillage both the recent and the not-so-recent past in the creation of their art, robbing the past of styles and forms encountered in art school. Frequently these impressions and ideas are mixed with others found in the craft traditions of the area, or are melded with images drawn from local poetic traditions, even from indigenous myths. The traditions of these men and women include a regional folklore in which can be found beauty, weirdness, humor, power, lyricism, even sensuality. Art Rosenbaum, Andy Nasisse, Ke Francis, Jr., among others, attest to the rich potpourri of folkloric experience that nurtures their creative energies.

How, then, shall we categorize what has emerged? How shall we deal with the multiplicity of images, styles, techniques, concerns? For purposes of the exhibition, the works selected have been grouped in the following categories:

Images of the Land
Images of People: Their (ordinary or, to us, extraordinary) Lives, Occupations, Preoccupations
Images Incorporating Myth, Totem, Folklore, Reverie, and Private Visions
Works of Art on Paper (which participate in any or all of the above, but which, when grouped in this category, seem to exhibit a special strength)

Images of the Land

These have emerged so strongly that one might be tempted to speak of a landscape school except that the term "school" implies some conscious, or at least casual, interaction, some discussion or interchange. There is, rather, an intimation in these images that it is the omnipresence of the mountains and the special quality of their light that brings about a preoccupation with this art form. Artist Jerry L. Noe, who is represented in the exhibition by a carved and painted mountain landscape (confined within a wooden box) that is spanned by a neon rainbow (fig. 2), speaks of the physical environment of the mountains. Raised in Appalachia, he daily saw "The sun rise over the mountains." In his work "the natural undulating arches of the mountain landscape have repeatedly cropped up . . . , often in an unconscious way, regardless of what medium I worked in

1. Lowell Hayes, detail (front view)
A T.V.A. Commonplace, 1980, cat. no. 40.

2. Jerry L. Noe, *Mountain Landscape with Rainbow*, 1980, cat. no. 75.

3. Lester F. Pross, *Woodlot*, 1973, cat. no. 78.

and what my conscious goals were at the time." Lester F. Pross (fig. 3) speaks of Kentucky's horizons, which "go with me. I see them from a distance, with a horizon view, rather than intimately and from the valleys. I like the larger view, the sense of the variety and order of forms and rhythms, the boldness and subtleties and colors, the large shapes and flattened spaces. . . . I live in these mountains, and they are my paintings." Although the landscape paintings of Victor Huggins (cat. no. 44) are composed of highly simplified, large-scale, sometimes embossed forms, he does not fail to observe the "undulating, sensuous form" of the mountains, and the "metamorphic, ephemeral" quality of their light as important factors in the development of this work. Betty G. Warner (fig. 4) speaks of the ways in which life in Appalachia has affected her angle of vision as she looks up through treetops or down at the valley floor from an exhilarating summit. Appalachia has taught her to look for visual surprises, often of an intimate character—"one last fern sheltered by rocks against the coming winter, the geometry of a cluster of farm buildings, the calligraphy of a sassafras grove at the edge of the meadow."

While some of the artists take a more traditional approach to landscape (Henry J. Drexler), others (for example, Huggins, Ippolito, Noe, and James K. Loveless) have produced works that freely borrow from the styles and sensibilities of the recent past to produce works more closely related to mainstream currents of modern American art than to conventional academic representation. Their imagery, often composed of striking, simplified forms and frequently enlivened by richly textured brushwork, is strongly individual, admirably suited to the revitalization of what many would regard as a traditionally realistic, perhaps moribund, art form. Still others express their feeling for landscape forms through the use of an unconventional medium (the ceramic landscapes of Ted Metz of Alabama; Lowell Hayes's room hanging—a work composed on three 36-inch hollow-core birch doors hinged to move in a Z fashion and adorned with paint, fibers, scraps of rags, and other materials too numerous to specify).

4. Betty G. Warner, *Amish Farmstead, Sundown*, 1979, cat. no. 104.

5. Angelo Ippolito, *Winter Landscape*,
1977–78, cat. no. 45.

Sometimes these men have approached landscape with whimsy; more often their art has been accomplished in ways that are richly romantic in their impulse and effect. Always they have painted with great ingenuity and inventiveness, creating imaginative, personal, deeply lyrical works. Their images of the land remain some of the most powerful works in the exhibition, lingering on, teasing our memory, awakening vague yearnings and desires.

Images of People: Their Lives, Occupations, Preoccupations

In overlooking or neglecting the reductive, nonobjective thrust of much modern art, many artists tend to place primary emphasis on narrative or associative qualities. This becomes apparent in the work of the artists drawn to images of the people of Appalachia and their lives. Frequently the presentation is straightforward. Mary Shelley's painted carving of the *Busy Bee Diner* (fig. 6), where she herself often stops for supper, is peopled with characters and figures familiar to the artist. She says that she had never known that she could draw, but when her father sent her a carved picture he had made of her as a little girl, she

6. Mary Shelley, *Busy Bee Diner*, 1980, cat. no. 90.

liked it so much she did one of her own. "At that time I was trying to be a writer, so naturally I took a story out of my life and set it down in picture form. Soon I had so much more reaction to my 'picture' stories that I stopped writing and kept carving."

Caryl Jones-Sylvester's eight-foot-long painted sculpture entitled *Suppertime* (fig. 7)—a constructed assemblage of wood, steel, aluminum, brass, plaster, and paint—is a nearly life-size depiction of the trailer culture she has known, a life that in its mobility she perceives as being a continuation of that of the "Romanian gypsies moving east to west, pilgrims crossing the westward sea to a new world, pioneers traveling toward the sunset in covered wagons." She regards her work as a historical document—a sort of oral history transposed into visual

7. Caryl Jones-Sylvester, detail (front view), *Suppertime*, 1981, cat. no. 51.

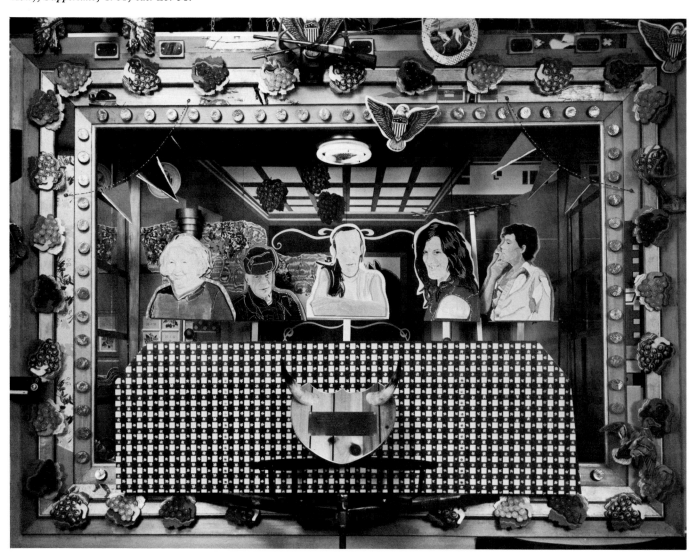

8. David "Blue" Lamm, *Roof Collapse*, 1978, cat. no. 60.

form—and has painstakingly collected more than 500 pages of transcribed interviews with trailer people, drawing inspiration and information from them so that in a quite literal sense of the word she may "build their story" for us to see. *Suppertime*, then, emerges as a work of archetypal strength—funky, joyous, imaginative, inventive, vulgar (to the uninitiated), and bursting with life.

The simple, storytelling aspects of these works are matched in directness by the strong polemic implied in the paintings of two men, David "Blue" Lamm and Andrew Mitchell Willis of the Miner's Art Group. Formed in 1975 in Belle, West Virginia, because, according to the group's pamphlet, the artists "felt the need to interpret through art . . . the concerns and aspirations of the people in the coal field," the group organizes art shows that travel throughout the state. It also encourages the participation of other amateur artists, for, as the pamphlet forthrightly states, "most of our artists are self-taught." Blue Lamm (fig. 8), one of the cofounders of the group, wants to show "the struggle of miners . . . for a better life" and does so with images of inflammatory power drawn both from communal memory and personal experience. His miners take on mythic dimensions, seemingly presented to us with the simple conviction that strong beliefs will find strong forms. His paintings do not prove him wrong.

The preoccupations of everyday can also be quiet and domestic, introspective, private. Carolyn C. Sanders-Turner has come in recent years to appreciate the traditional art forms and handicrafts of women. Crocheting and quilting are now often incorporated in her works, "both symbolically and realistically." Most of her paintings deal with women, "their varied and hidden existences, fantasies,

19

detail

9. Carolyn C. Sanders-Turner, *Forgotten Treasures*, 1980, cat. no. 87.

and trappings." *Forgotten Treasures* (fig. 9) intertwines these preoccupations in a work rich in texture, both of surface and of association. Critic Lucy Lippard has written of the concern of many contemporary women artists for emotion and for autobiographical fiber in their works; of the self-confidence with which they now paint as women seeking their own personal, even generic identity. They no longer attempt to paint "just like a man," are no longer flattered when they are praised for having done so. Through the images they employ they deliberately suggest their need to reach out beyond the self-contained art object for meaning, context, and ties with society, the past, and their inner selves.

Jean Thickens Francis's works of art on paper—works created with paper she herself has made with the use of plant materials near at hand, works often created in the form of letters, embellished with porcelain messages and beribboned with silk—are predicated on this act of reaching out and emphasize these ties.

> . . . when one lives in the country, communication is much more intuitive. . . . The images, visions, and dreams that we would so quickly share in a city must wait until a letter can be written. . . . The messages I send to those far away are ones of a peaceful dawn, a quiet moment in the wet woods, or the quality and patterns of light. . . .

20

10. Jean Thickens Francis, *Rainbow Fallout,* 1980, cat. no. 33.

21

The tiny details or wild expanse of nature are the fabrics that I dye, tear, and pour into paper. The moments that I wish to share become porcelain stamps, letters, and gifts. The photoetchings are glimpses of friends and family and places loved as memory gives them back to us in her strange collaged fashion. The threads of silk or dyed cords are used as symbols of "ties," bonds that revitalize and reinforce like the rain. Everything in these collages relates to what is most real to me—our human spirit and its ties (with nature and each other) and the unbelieveable variations with which we use them, communicate them, and celebrate them.

Her work, so difficult to define, equally at home under several of the rubrics we have chosen for discussion, strongly partakes of reverie and private vision. At times it can also suggest a creative area deepened in its significance by a strong reliance on myth and folklore.

Images Incorporating Myth, Totem, Folklore, Reverie, and Private Visions

I think artists who have chosen to represent the values of their people . . . represent a new thrust in American art. It may be that in our short history we have covered the surface of our artistic concerns to our satisfaction and that some real depth needs to be cut in our cultural topography.

Ke Francis, Jr., Tupelo, Mississippi

While contemporary artists in other sections of the country have in recent years frequently spoken of ritual and myth, longing for a time when strong beliefs were collectively held by large segments of the population, the Appalachian artist has been able to mine the widely held folkloric and religious traditions of his own region. The Reverend Howard Finster, "man of vision," environmental artist, preacher, singer, and banjo player from Georgia, paints with personal conviction and biblical authority, apocalyptically calling us to prepare for a Second Coming in works full of wild fantasy, part biblical, part science fiction in character. Thomas J. Golya of New York State combs his rural environment to collect the materials—wood, stone, animal skeletons, and the like—that he uses in his sculpture (fig. 11), as does William Beckwith of Mississippi. Golya says the folkloric and Indian history of the region "titillate" his imagination to bring forth totemic images of weirdness and beauty. Their primitive quality seems far removed from the gently humorous porcelain sculptures of Frank Fleming who, with disarming seriousness, explores the world of animals that he learned to trust in childhood. The inhabitants of this world have come to seem his true "neighbors," and he admits his enduring suspicions concerning man. Graced with anthropomorphic aplomb, his animals lounge in chairs, recline on sofas, engage in musical recitals and recitations, or silently commune. But they do not seem amusing to their creator who, far from making the slightest conscious attempt at wit, is only concerned with the empathetic presentation of their images and characters. Humor is in the eye of the beholder; yet somehow the mood of

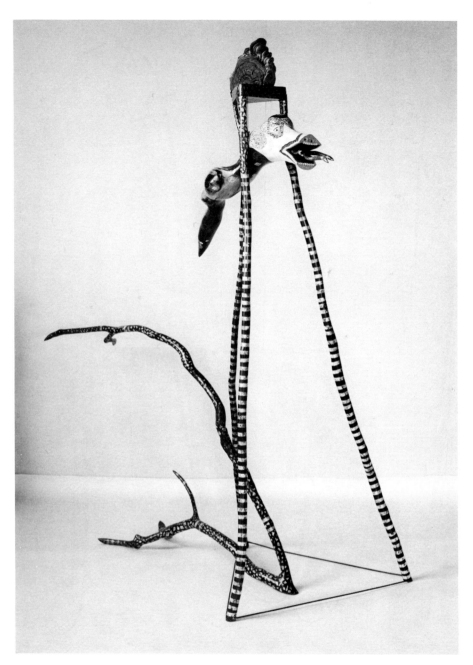

11. Thomas J. Golya, *Happiness/Madness Landscape Segment (An Allegory)*, 1979, cat. no. 36.

Fleming's work (fig. 12) is one of civilized irony and gentle playfulness. Victorian children's books such as the Beatrice Potter stories are never very far away from our minds as we view his works, despite the backwoods, "down-home" feeling of his animal characters, their furniture, and the fantasy environment created by them. Another artist, Nall of Arab, Alabama, exploits the lingering Victorian aspects of Southern society in his "Alice in Wonderland" lithographs (fig. 13), a series in which he explicitly satirizes his neighbors in his hometown while utilizing them as models for a surreal presentation of characters drawn from the famous book.

12. Frank Fleming, *A Dog's Painful
Search for Knowledge*, 1980, cat. no. 31.

13. Nall, righthand print, *Alice II*, from
"Metamorphosis Series," 1977, cat. no.
70.

14. Ron Isaacs, *Black Dress with Scissors*, 1978, cat. no. 46.

Nall's visions are acerbic but no more private than those of Ron Isaacs (fig. 14), whose dresses—ingenious trompe l'oeil constructions of thinly carved and painted plywood simulating women's clothing from days gone by—also suggest their own environments, their own vague stories. Isaacs states that he "stresses formal considerations and visual relationships over other kinds of content" in his work. We must take the artist at his word, but, as he himself admits, his use of antique clothing as imagery suggests the "feel" of the Appalachian country, "the continued life of its past in its present." And, finally, he says that his choice of subject matter is rooted in "complex reasons" and "past associations" that he does not fully understand. His ordinary, period clothes, which populate our present space, seem as poised between reality and dream as the ordinary people created by Ronald Kroutel of Athens, Ohio. Kroutel's people (fig. 15) are not, however, symbolic evocations of other eras. They run, float, and even levitate in frozen moments of ordinary action, thereby taking on a quality of mystery and magic.

Whatever their specific character, the images presented in this exhibition are born of the solitude and loneliness of a once-remote region and of a culture that has traditionally honored idiosyncratic, highly personal ways of life. The original white settlers in the area came centuries ago. Largely of English, Scottish, and Irish ancestery, they revered family and clan. "Who one was" derived less from one's personal character and habits than from one's family. To "know" someone was to know his or her blood ties—grandparents, aunts, uncles, cousins, remote kin. What a person's family was depended on its history. The inhabitants of Appalachia were inexorably embedded in these twin elements of fate: blood ties and family history; with them as supports and guarantees of personal worth, however, great license could be given to eccentricity and to the free play of imagination in all its strangeness, weirdness, and beauty. In isolation, this imagination was inevitably turned inward. F. Clark Stewart (fig. 16), an artist from Knoxville, Tennessee, notes that the compelling artistic current, the creative bent of the area, is strongly directed toward the development of private visions, the creation of interior environments, the exploration of complex,

15. Ron Kroutel, *Animus I: Athleticism*, 1974, cat. no. 57.

16. F. Clark Stewart, *Darkpool*, 1978, cat.
no. 97.

focused inner spaces. He is but one of many artists who investigate these inscapes.

Works of Art on Paper

Works of art on paper, by virtue of their special nature, constitute a separate
section of the exhibition, even though each of the works may participate in one
or more of the categories already mentioned. A significant number of these artists make their own paper, sometimes deliberately including tangible remnants
of their physical surroundings in their work. Vera M. Dickerson (fig.17) speaks
of the grasses, leaves, pressed flowers, even feathers from quail and turkey buzzards that she includes in her handmade papers. After manufacturing the paper,
she physically manipulates its surfaces—stitching, gluing, tearing, laminating,
spattering, drawing, and painting. She aims to unite "color, tactile surface, visual texture, and line" in her work. Adrienne Anderson shares similar concerns.
A number of her recent handmade paper constructions are wordless "books" in
which calligraphic patches of color visually present not a story but her feelings
and emotions, her joyous response to such simple everyday occurences as gardens in bloom (fig. 18). Her books are works of reverie and private associations.
Precious objects made from mundane elements, they possess the traditional tactile immediacy and intimacy of books, as well as their inwardness.

Works of art on paper need not be small in scope or exclusively intimate in feeling. Steven Barbash's great eight-foot drawing *Dog Watching, Raystown River*

27

17. Vera M. Dickerson, *Fable*, 1979, cat. no. 17.

(fig. 19) is both panoramic and intimate in quality, to a contradictory degree. Barbash, a native New Yorker who has adopted Appalachia and lived within its borders during his entire adult working life, approaches his art with the sophistication gained from training at Yale under Josef Albers and from a thoroughgoing knowledge of both Western and Eastern traditions in the visual arts. His *Raystown River* is a kind of visual expedition or reconnaissance of this particular area, encompassing both sweeping vista and minute observation of the sticks, stones, and twigs of the natural landscape. Each detail is noted with such precision that, despite the overall grand view, the ultimate effect is one of glint and glimmer, of dazzling surface sparkle. And, within one of the pockets formed by the plunging slopes of the river banks and the swirling forest thickets, sits a dog, the lone participant in Barbash's exaltation of nature.

Barbash's huge drawing is a fitting one to use in summarizing many of the tendencies discussed in the works of other artists in this exhibition. Its largeness of scale, combined with the traditional intimacy of the medium of drawing, presents only one of the many visual surprises and contradictions to be encountered in this exhibition. A work demonstrating enormous technical control and great visual erudition, *Raystown River* is direct in its approach and effect, forthright and seemingly simple in its imagery and subject matter. Here, as with many artists throughout this exhibition and throughout generations of American painting, images of the land and of the wilderness are of enduring concern. The

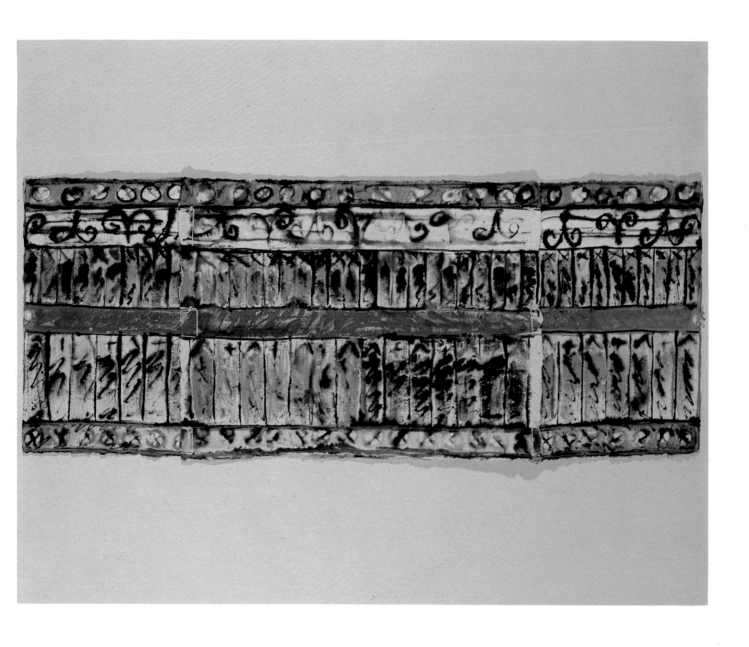

18. Adrienne Anderson, *Summer Garden*,
1980, cat. no. 1.

19. Steven A. Barbash, detail, *Dog Watching, Raystown River*, 1978–80, cat. no. 3.

more closely we examine the work, the more we realize, however, that it is far from simple. It is made up of an infinite series of nooks and crannies, of pockets vibrating with visual interest, each leading the eye with great sophistication and cunning onward to greater involvement, greater delight. Although traditional in its choice of subject matter, it demonstrates a total awareness of the past thirty years of contemporary art. It is the work of a man who has immersed himself in his immediate environment, yet has preserved to the highest degree a sense of his own individuality.

Such works provide us with a new image of Appalachia; no longer an area of our country isolated or cut off from the outer world, it becomes one in which traditions, appreciated and perceived by knowing eyes, are creatively incorporated into new and diverse works of art. These works at their best wield powers as persuasive as those of this region of serious people and of the singing hills, mountains, and glens from which they come. From them we learn that the art of Appalachia is one to which the mind may turn for needed sustenance. Like the mountain retreats of the region, these works of art can act to restore, freshen, and quicken our spirits.

Lenders to the Exhibition

Adrienne Anderson, Birmingham, Alabama

American Folklife Center, Library of Congress, Washington, D.C.

Steven A. Barbash, Cortland, New York

Mr. and Mrs. John Haynes Barnhart, Chillicothe, Ohio

William Beckwith, Greenwood, Mississippi

Birmingham Art Association, Alabama

Borgenicht Gallery, New York, New York

Noyes Capehart, Boone, North Carolina

Gayle and Andrew Camden, Detroit, Michigan

Capricorn Galleries, Bethesda, Maryland

Helen Z. Chilton, Charleston, West Virginia

Victor Colby, Groton, New York

David R. Craft, Chattanooga, Tennessee

Anne Clark Culbert, Athens, Ohio

Raymond DeFazio, Jeannette, Pennsylvania

Charles de Limur, San Francisco, California

Vera M. Dickerson, Roanoke, Virginia

Neil Di Teresa, Berea, Kentucky

Henry J. Drexler, Norwich, New York

Charles J. Eldred, Binghamton, New York

Steve Ferguson, Boone, North Carolina

Fisher Brothers and the Prudential Insurance Company of America, New York, New York

John P. Forest, D.D.S., Annandale, Virginia

Jean Thickens Francis, Tupelo, Mississippi

Ke Francis, Jr., Tupelo, Mississippi

Myron Friedman, Shawnee Mission, Kansas

Thomas J. Golya, Forestville, New York

Haber/Theodore Gallery, New York, New York

Lowell Hayes, Valle Crucis, North Carolina

Nancy Hoffman Gallery, New York, New York

Lonnie B. Holley, Birmingham, Alabama

Jewell and Robert Hoogstoel, Toledo, Ohio

Vernon F. Howell, Barboursville, West Virginia

Huntsville Museum of Art, Alabama

Judy V. Jones, Spartanburg, South Carolina

Caryl Jones-Sylvester, Cameron Mills, New York

Katherine Kadish, Binghamton, New York

Edward Kellogg, Chattanooga, Tennessee

Phyllis Kern, San Francisco, California

John W. Kortlander, Athens, Ohio

Kraushaar Galleries, New York, New York

Ron Kroutel, Athens, Ohio

David "Blue" Lamm, Rand, West Virginia

Edward J. Lee, Norwich, New York

James K. Loveless, Hamilton, New York

David A. Lucas, Cromona, Kentucky

Stephen Q. Luckett, Halltown, West Virginia

Richard Lutzke, Hagerstown, Maryland

Stephen Mader, Syracuse, New York

Daniel D. Maye and Phillip S. Cooke, Louisville, Kentucky

Monique Knowlton Gallery, New York, New York

Marilyn Morton, Chattanooga, Tennessee

Paul Munson, Radford, Virginia

Museums at Sunrise, Charleston, West Virginia

Andy Nasisse, Athens, Georgia

Jerry L. Noe, Chapel Hill, North Carolina

Pilot Freight Carriers, Winston-Salem, North Carolina

Lester F. Pross, Berea, Kentucky

Robert T. Reedy, Mantachie, Mississippi

David L. Riffle, Poca, West Virginia

Roanoke Museum of Fine Arts, Virginia

Michael Rogers, University, Mississippi

Edward Rogge, Kilmichael, Mississippi

Art Rosenbaum, Athens, Georgia

Richard and Lois Rosenthal, Cincinnati, Ohio

Mary and Cy Rutledge, Chillicothe, Ohio

Carolyn C. Sanders-Turner, Beckley, West Virginia

Elizabeth W. Shumacker, Chattanooga, Tennessee

Barry Spilberg, Chicago, Illinois

John Spofforth, Athens, Ohio

F. Clark Stewart, Knoxville, Tennessee

Joe W. Thrasher, Adamsville, Alabama

Mrs. Alice Townsend, Signal Mountain, Tennessee

T. M. Townsend, Galveston, Texas

Dr. & Mrs. Willis Trammell, Charleston, West Virginia

Dr. Thomas Tyra, Cullowhee, North Carolina

Barry Vance, Brandywine, West Virginia

Helen Johnston Vaughn, Huntsville, Alabama

Clune Walsh, Detroit, Michigan

Mr. & Mrs. George S. Weikart, Jr., Hagerstown, Maryland

20. John W. Kortlander, *Appalachian Landscape*, 1980, cat. no. 55.

Catalogue of the Exhibition

Unless otherwise indicated, dimensions are in inches, followed, in parentheses, by centimeters. Height precedes width and depth. The entries are arranged alphabetically by last names of artists. The works were lent by the artists unless the name of another lender is included.

In only a few instances are illustrations in the front section repeated in this part of the catalogue. Entries that are not illustrated here are marked with an asterisk (*), and a figure number (second line) is provided.

Adrienne Anderson

Born in Richmond, Virginia, 1949. Received B.F.A. 1971 and M.F.A. 1973 from University of Georgia, Athens. Taught 1973–76 at University of Montevallo, Alabama. Has been included in numerous juried and invitational group exhibitions. Since 1975 has had one-woman exhibitions at galleries throughout the South. Is in many collections, including, in Alabama, Huntsville Museum of Art and Montgomery Museum of Fine Arts. Taught 1976–80 at Alabama School of Fine Arts, Birmingham, and currently is cochairperson of its Department of Visual Arts.

1.
Summer Garden   1980
* figure 18 (color)
watercolor and acrylic on handmade paper
portfolio and three leaves:
portfolio 23 × 16½ (58.4 × 41.9)
each leaf 15½ × 20½ (39.4 × 52.1)

2.
New Hope   1980
watercolor and acrylic on handmade paper
six-page book:
each page 10 × 6½ (25.4 × 16.5)

Living in the foothills of Appalachia does not have to make an artist an isolated idiot, blithely working, unaware of the outside world and unaware of current trends in today's art world. It does allow one a certain sense of free choice to accept, or reject, certain current principles, or it could allow an artist to mainstream on his or her own. I have rejected certain academic painting principles for something more immediate and direct and for a more immediate and direct reaction and response from the viewer.

Living and working in Virginia, Tennessee, North Carolina, Georgia, and Alabama have kept me relatively free from certain distracting influences, real or imagined, in major urban environs, allowing or freeing me to use my own senses and judgments. The pace of life is slower here, providing for more liberty to pursue my own direction—but then, the support for the arts is much less here than in a major city. The loneliness and the idea that there are few people looking at art are depressing, but this situation is slowly being rectified by the founding of local art organizations.

The actual influences of Appalachia on my work are difficult to pin down. My use of simple iconographics, primitive forms, and bright, clear colors could very well be influenced by living here. My use of handmade paper, primitively fabricated, and my making of rather simple, bound books could possibly be a part of this sensibility. But the important fact is that it really does not matter where one is working or creating, or thinking, as long as the act of making art is happening.

Steven A. Barbash

Born in New York City, 1933. Studied summer 1951 at Art Students League, New York City; received B.A. 1955 from Bard College, Annandale-on-Hudson, New York, and M.F.A. 1960 from School of Art and Architecture, Yale University, New Haven, Connecticut. Numerous awards and fellowships include John Bard scholarship, 1951–55; Yale University scholarship, 1958–60; and Danforth Foundation grant, 1961. Has exhibited widely in both group and one-man exhibitions. Is represented in USSR in Pushkin Museum, Moscow; in New York State in Herbert F. Johnson Museum of Art, Cornell University, Ithaca; and in Washington, D.C., in Corcoran Gallery of Art and National Museum of American Art, Smithsonian Institution. Taught at Juniata College, Huntington, Pennsylvania, 1960–69. Since 1970 has been professor of art and chairman of Art Department, State University of New York at Cortland.

3.
Dog Watching, Raystown River 1978–80
see also figure 19
pencil on paper
48 × 96 (121.9 × 243.8)

I *chose a small rural college for my first teaching post because I felt my work would benefit from my living amongst the themes with which I was dealing. The year following my arrival at Juniata College I bought a very isolated farm high in the nearby mountains, established my studio, and worked there for the next nine years. I visited New York City regularly. I was able to stay in touch, yet separate.*

In 1969 work was started on a very large dam and lake in the area adjacent to my farm, which was selected for use as a recreational area. At this time I was offered the chairmanship of the Art Department of the State University of New York at Cortland, so in 1970 I moved to this area in upstate New York in which I still live.

In 1977 I began work on the current drawing series. At first I used ordinary formats and scales. As the demands of the new compositional idea grew, however, the format expanded.

Steven A. Barbash

The work is the result of my stay in these mountains. Dog
Watching, Raystown River *is the twelfth time I have used
as the primary theme of a work this particular spot along the
river, even though it is now 200 feet below the surface of
Raystown Lake.*

4.
Yellow Perch   1979
etching with chine-collé on paper
36½ × 23½ (92.7 × 59.7)

36

William Beckwith

Born in Greenville, Mississippi, 1952. Received B.F.A. 1974 and M.F.A. 1976 from University of Mississippi, University. Has been included in exhibitions and is represented in collections throughout the United States; has won awards for sculpture. Established Vulcan Studios, Mississippi's first commercial fine-art bronze foundry, in 1976. Recipient of grant from the Mississippi Department of Humanities, 1981. Currently shares a studio in Oxford, Mississsippi.

5.
Terrapin Cruiser   1980
bronze
$9 \times 9 \times 7$ ($22.9 \times 22.9 \times 17.8$)

Living in Appalachia has had a unique influence on both the content and the subject matter of my sculpture. The rich folklore of the region has been an invaluable inheritance to me as an artist. The yarns and tales of every child's grandfather found their way to the campfire of my childhood.

The influence of the nature of the region has had a solid effect on the subject matter of my sculpture also. The thousands of acres of natural wilderness have been a lifelong fascination and inspiration. Some of my fantasies are drawn from childhood memories. Terrapin Cruiser, *however, involves adult fantasy. This is achieved through the employment of natural bone shapes, i.e., racoon shoulder blades and sections from a dog skull, combined to give a feeling of science fiction, as in the movie* Star Wars.

Being a professional artist in the Appalachia region has given me a true sense of uniqueness and importance. The local people are amazed at someone's making a profession of art. There is a great satisfaction in being appreciated as an artist here, if not always understood. I find the region rich in every important way. Every time I question my surroundings, I remind myself of the times I stood in line at a New York gallery with my portfolio of slides under my arm, waiting with countless other artists for my turn to feel totally unappreciated and unneeded.

Noyes Capehart

Born in Nashville, Tennessee, 1933. Received B.A. 1958 from Auburn University, Alabama, and M.A. 1963 from University of Missouri, Columbia. Taught at University of Missouri 1963–67 and University of Mississippi, University, 1967–69. Has participated in many major exhibitions in United States and has won awards for painting and printmaking. Was included in "National Print Annual" at The Brooklyn Museum, New York, 1964, and traveling exhibition "Extraordinary Realities," which opened at Whitney Museum of American Art, New York City, in 1973. Since 1969 has taught drawing and printmaking at Appalachian State University, Boone, North Carolina, and in 1981 was appointed assistant dean of its College of Fine and Applied Arts.

As a resident of this part of North Carolina for over ten years, I have become aware of many aspects of Appalachia. I have seen and known degrees of economic hardships, I have experienced and enjoyed the folk art of this part of the country, and I have witnessed the intensity with which persons of this area meet their daily experiences. Living in this area has enabled me to view the more sophisticated and urban sectors of the country with a patience and objectivity that has helped me in realizing my values and the values of my family. The influence of Appalachia has not been a direct one—a force, for example—that shows its power in my work; rather, I have become sensitized through the Appalachia experience. I would like to believe that the fundamental integrity of simple mountain folk has permeated my outlook and, most important, my posture as an artist.

6.
An Evil Conversation   1976
From "Evil Conversations Series"
mixed media on paper
26 × 30 (66 × 76.2)

Helen Z. Chilton

7.
Apples 1980
watercolor on paper
35 × 48 (88.9 × 121.9)

Born in Bethlehem, Pennsylvania, 1946. Received B.F.A. 1968 from Denison University, Granville, Ohio. In Charleston, West Virginia, taught art to fourth through sixth graders, spring 1980; led adult education classes in advanced watercolor, winter 1981. Has exhibited locally, including two one-woman exhibitions at University of Charleston, West Virginia, 1978 and 1979. Prizes include Award of Excellence, "Annual Rhododendron State Outdoor Art and Crafts Festival," Charleston, 1979.

I am a product of Appalachia. I have never lived anywhere else except to attend school. I try to use my knowledge of design, composition, and color, gained during college and cultivated during the past years, to create work that represents me and my environment. As I view the world around me, my paintings are a statement of that world. In college I assimilated whatever my environment suggested as important; therefore, I painted ideas and theories, abstract compositions, and models. Now I paint my garden—plants, insects, flowers, fruit; my found objects—hats, tools, old toys; my home and family; house plants; collectibles. My painting tends to be "seasonal"; that is, whatever is in season or available at the time. I try to express the essence of my interest in my subject matter. The all-consuming physical and mental involvement of transferring my impressions of the subject to the paper is as important to me as the product. My isolation from the "mainstream" of American art has served the purpose of consolidating my interest in my immediate surroundings. Some day I may feel the need for more outside stimulation, but right now I find a consuming challenge all around me.

Marvin S. Coats

Born in Dallas, Texas, 1943. Received B.S. in art and psychology 1969 from East Texas State University, Commerce, and M.F.A. 1971 from University of Oklahoma, Norman. Taught at University of Wisconsin at Whitewater, serving 1971–73 as director of its Crossman Gallery. Served as gallery director and assistant professor of art, Humboldt State University, Arcata, California, 1974–76. Has participated in numerous group and one-man exhibitions, including one-man show at The Southeastern Center for Contemporary Art, Winston-Salem, North Carolina, 1979. Among numerous prizes is Museum Purchase Award, "Eleventh Midwest Biennial," Joslyn Art Museum, Omaha, Nebraska. Since 1976 has taught sculpture and design at Wake Forest University, Winston-Salem.

I have a very strong sense of place and being, and I've definitely been influenced by all the places I've lived. I feel very good about the development of my art during the five years I have lived in North Carolina. The influence of this area is less visually obvious in my work, but then I've become more adept at assimilating the things around me. Since I've been here, I've definitely taken advantage of the opportunities to work and grow as an artist.

It is difficult to describe, in a few words, what my art is about, but it is basically concerned with the use of word/ image juxtapositions that can be interpreted in both a literal and symbolic way, and that have multiple connotations. Much of my work is autobiographical and narrative. I love to tell stories, which are usually derived from personal experiences and from my relationships with friends. Recently this has been one of the most influential components in my work. Not every piece is about a particular experience or story, but the pieces are cyclical in that they relate to and from one another and come from within me.

8.
Housecat   1979
painted wood
$18 \times 11 \times 12$ ($45.7 \times 27.9 \times 30.5$)
Lent by T. M. Townsend, Galveston, Texas

Victor Colby

Born in Frankfort, Indiana, 1917. Received A.B. 1948 from Indiana University at Bloomington and M.F.A. 1950 from Cornell University, Ithaca, New York. Has had numerous one-man exhibitions at, among others, Munson-Williams-Proctor Institute, Utica, New York; Hewitt Gallery, New York City; The Contemporary Gallery, New York City; Cornell University; State University of New York at Cortland; and Jane Haslem Gallery, Washington, D.C. Has participated in group exhibitions at The Art Institute of Chicago, Illinois; Allan Stone Gallery, New York City; Roberson Center for The Arts and Sciences, Binghamton, New York; The Museum of Modern Art, New York City, and Albright-Knox Art Gallery, Buffalo, New York. Since 1950 has been faculty member, Department of Fine Arts, College of Architecture, Art, and Planning, Cornell University.

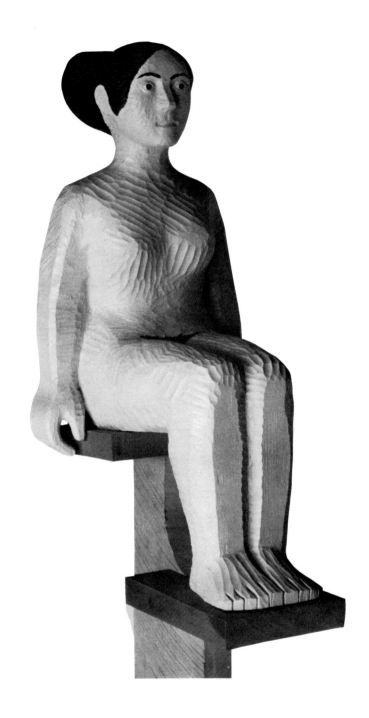

9.
Seated Pink Nude   1974
carved, partially painted wood
76 × 20 × 50 (193 × 50.8 × 127)

10.
Small Icarus   1964
carved, partially painted wood
37 × 12 × 15 (94 × 30.5 × 38.1)

41

David R. Craft

Born in Elberton, Georgia, 1945. Received
B.S. 1968 from East Tennessee State University, Johnson City. Served as military
photographer, United States Air Force,
1969–70. Among numerous exhibitions are
"The Contemporary Miniature," Drawing
National, Ann Arbor, Michigan, 1977; and
"Personal Statements," Drawing Invitational, The Southeastern Center for Contemporary Art, Winston-Salem, North
Carolina, 1979. Has won numerous museum purchase awards and is widely collected. Since 1975 has taught drawing,
painting, and composition at Hunter Museum School of Art, Chattanooga, Tennessee.

11.
Post Meridian—Late Bloom 1977
graphite on paper
18 × 21 (45.7 × 53.3)

12.
Summer Solstice—Light Collectors 1981
oil on panel
image 6 × 7¾ (15.2 × 19.7)

The earliest years of my life were spent in Tennessee and Georgia. Because this was a pretelevision era, I spent a great deal of time outside, and because I lived in a small town (Kingsport, Tennessee), I was more exposed to landscape than to the city.

Until I spent two years in the Northwest (Spokane, Washington), I believe that I took for granted the type of atmosphere we have in the South. I know that I was very aware of the hazy softness of the light when I returned to Tennessee in 1970. It was at this time I started working more from the land than from the figure. I found that the more I isolated things of personal attraction in the region, the more I felt I had to translate these things in a specific technique. The more I thought in terms of transparency, the more I isolated elements in the subject matter. Everything fits for me now. I find recall from my past to be a very strong source of imagery—as are my dreams, which are more and more concerned with fantasy landscapes ordered around the elements of transparency. I believe that if I had grown up in any other part of the world, I would still have been attracted to landscape. The fact that I live in the South is a plus for me. I feel that it offers a great deal of variety when compared to other regions.

13.
Summer Solstice—Vertical View 1981
oil on panel
image 7¾ × 6 (19.7 × 15.2)

George Ayers Cress

Born in Anniston, Alabama, 1921. Received B.F.A. 1942 and M.F.A. 1949 from University of Georgia, Athens. Taught at University of Tennessee at Knoxville, 1949–51. Has participated in numerous group exhibitions at, among others, Pennsylvania Academy of The Fine Arts, Philadelphia; and The Butler Institute of American Art, Youngstown, Ohio. Has had one-man exhibitions at Addison Gallery of American Art, Andover, Massachusetts, and Hunter Museum of Art, Chattanooga, Tennessee, where work was given a twenty-year retrospective. Works are included in The High Museum of Art, Atlanta, Georgia; Birmingham Museum of Art, Alabama; The Mint Museum of Art, Charlotte, North Carolina; and many others. Since 1951 has taught at University of Tennessee, Chattanooga, and is currently Guerry professor and head of the university's Art Department.

For over thirty years I have painted in the Appalachian region. As a landscape painter primarily, I have derived most of my inspiration, subject matter, and motifs from this region. When I was a student during the late 1930s and 1940s, I sketched and painted in the mountains of northeast Georgia. During the 1950s and 1960s, I used this subject matter, as well as that from other areas of Appalachia, in a more structured way—often in a semiabstract style. Of great importance to me were the effects of light and the changing seasons, which constituted my point of departure for varying formats and palettes.

In recent years I have returned to on-the-spot painting, making few changes when the canvases are back in the studio. Such paintings, executed in perhaps two hours, have an immediacy and special meaning for me. The years I devoted to consciously developing my compositions have been abandoned for a more instinctive ordering of the shapes and colors. My use in future of patterns and motifs from the Appalachian landscape will, I expect, result in a more abstract quality in my work.

14.
Ravine   1977
oil on canvas
22 × 28 (55.9 × 71.1)
Lent by Marilyn Morton, Chattanooga, Tennessee

Anne Clark Culbert

Born in New York City, 1921. Received B.A. 1941 from Bennington College, Vermont, and M.A. 1944 from University of Michigan, Ann Arbor. As graduate special student, studied art at Ohio University, Athens, 1965–75. Taught art at Union Settlement, East Harlem, New York City, summer 1946; under National Endowment for the Arts "Artists in the Schools" program, taught art in city and county schools, Athens, Ohio, spring 1978 and 1979. Since 1965 has been Athens County (Ohio) 4H adviser in conservation and creative arts. Has exhibited locally.

15.
Summer Hotel   1978
ceramic
8 × 8 × 4 (20.3 × 20.3 × 10.2)

I *have been living in Appalachia for twenty-seven of my adult years, and during childhood spent many summers on my grandmother's farm in the northern panhandle of West Virginia. This environment has meant a great deal to me and must have affected my art in many complex ways. I especially feel that my childhood years, split as they were between the sophisticated culture of New York City and its environs and the far more basic, back-to-fundamentals life I led in West Virginia, made an extremely deep impression on me and my work. Today, of course, I use the landscape around Athens, Ohio, which I love, and take advantage in many ways of the cultural opportunities offered by Ohio University. But I think I especially have felt, here in southeastern Ohio, so close to West Virginia, a sense of coming home.*

Raymond DeFazio

Born in Point Marion, Pennsylvania, 1936. Received B.F.A. 1958 from Carnegie Institute of Technology (now Carnegie-Mellon University), Pittsburgh, Pennsylvania, and M. Ed. 1964 from Pennsylvania State University, University Park. Since 1962 has participated in "Associated Artists of Pittsburgh Annual Exhibition," Carnegie-Mellon University, and received Jury Award in 1966, 1970, 1973, and 1974. Participated 1967 and 1977 in "National Annual Midyear Show," The Butler Institute of American Art, Youngstown, Ohio. Received Purchase Prize in 1971 exhibition at The Westmoreland County Museum of Art, Greensburg, Pennsylvania, and had one-man exhibition there in 1978. Currently is associate professor, Seton Hill College, Greensburg. Lives in Jeannette, Pennsylvania.

I paint in order to examine and experience more deeply the miracle of life, the world that is within me and the world that is around me. My paintings are always records of the way these two worlds meet. For most of my life, the world that is around me has been western Pennsylvania, with all that this geographic area means in terms of climate, landscape, and people.

There was a time in my development as an artist when I tried to ignore my relationship to the land. I felt that advanced painting was inevitably bound up with abstraction, and spent a number of years exploring abstraction as a means of self-expression. But around 1966, I experienced a kind of crisis in my work. The theories of abstraction were intellectually stimulating, but I had to face up to the fact that something was going on inside me that would never be compatible with pure abstraction. I was painting abstractions out of my head, but my deepest instincts were pulling me to the land, not in its simplified geometric aspects, etc., but to its visual reality, its colors, shapes, and moods. I decided I could no longer fight the desire to paint bridges and clouds and hills and houses and the multitude of things that make up the western Pennsylvania landscape, the world around me. Above all, I realized that I could no longer fight my desire to paint light, which changes with each hour and each season, which binds all things on earth together in fleeting harmonies, and which more than anything else, awakens that world within me. I realized then, and I understand even more deeply now, that when I paint light, I am attempting a fusion of my two worlds. I am attempting to explore and to express my reality as a spiritual being.

16.
Nightfall, Allegheny Observatory   1978–79
oil on canvas
32 × 58¼ (81.3 × 148)

Vera M. Dickerson

Born in Radford, Virginia, 1946. Received B.A. 1968 from Radford University, and M.F.A. 1970 from American University, Washington, D.C. Taught at Radford University, 1970, 1971; Keuka College, Keuka Park, New York, 1970–72; Virginia Western Community College, Roanoke, Virginia, 1972–81; and has conducted numerous papermaking workshops. Has been included in exhibitions at The Southeastern Center for Contemporary Art, Winston-Salem, North Carolina, and Virginia Museum of Fine Arts, Richmond.

17.
Fable 1979
figure 17
mixed media on handmade paper
17 × 17 (43.2 × 43.2)

By birth and environment I am a product of the Appalachian area. Oral family history, old photograph albums, and quilts handed down from my great-grandmothers have combined to fashion some of my subject matter. I have developed a respect for these people as well as love for their crafted, pragmatic artistic expressions.

However, a more intangible influence asserts itself in the tactile surfaces of my work. I was introduced to handmade paper just over two years ago and have found it to be an incredibly responsive medium. Appalachia offers richness of leaf and flower forms, wild ranges of textures, and a softly filtered atmospheric light that is as gentle as the mountain slopes.

These surroundings extend to vegetable inclusions in my paper—grasses, leaves, pressed flowers, even feathers from quail and turkey buzzards. I can physically manipulate the surfaces by stitching and gluing, tearing, laminating, spattering, drawing and painting. I feel greedy in my wish to have color, tactile surface, visual texture, and line all in one. I have seen such a controlled chaos in the wealth of these elements just beyond my window that I recognize the source to be inexhaustible.

Critics have said that it is a feminine characteristic to be sensitive to surface. If so, I make no apologies. After finishing my formal education I realized that I was now working for myself and about myself. Nature is infinitely changeable. If art cannot be quite so varied, it should at least entertain the eye, not bore it. Mine is a sensuously aware, romantic approach fed by what I see each day. I am a romantic and have learned not only to live with it but even to enjoy it.

Neil Di Teresa

Born in Staten Island, New York, 1938.
Received B.S. 1959 from Pratt Institute,
Brooklyn, New York, and M.A. from
University of New Mexico, Albuquerque.
Was guest artist, John C. Campbell Folk
School, Brasstown, North Carolina, sum-
mers 1968 and 1969. Received Mellon
Foundation grant 1979–80 for study and
research in philosophy and English litera-
ture at University of Kent at Canterbury,
England. Received Seabury Award for Ex-
cellence in Teaching 1970 from Berea Col-
lege, Kentucky. Since 1970 has directed
"A Summer Puppetry Caravan for Appala-
chia," Berea College Cultural Outreach
Program. Has exhibited widely in both
United States and Europe. Since 1962 has
taught at Berea College, and is currently
professor of art there.

18.
Bird and Herd   1978
acrylic on canvas
36 × 36 (91.4 × 91.4)

*Kentucky is a composite of geographies: the plainslike west-
ern section, the rolling gentle green hills of the Bluegrass, the
raw-boned angularity of the mountains and the harshness of
their landscape. These generate a set of related attitudes about
life.*

*A New Yorker by birth, I spent my early life in a landscape
almost completely man-manipulated. This environment, too,
led me into attitudes and conclusions about life that defined
my work then: a sense of internal conflict and tension; a
harsh reality of blacks and grays; a desire for high technique
for its own sake; a personally aggressive stance—all points
and angles.*

*I have lived and worked in Kentucky since 1962 and during
these years experience and growing older in the mountains
have led me to some alternative conclusions: 1) Simplicity, especially in art, is a virtue; 2) communication on a personal
level feeds both the artist and his public; 3) concerns about
style or current vogue will leave an artist both lacking a personal style and hopelessly out of date; 4) the means of art—
the skill, the media manipulating, the image-building process,
the application of intellect and idea in the struggle to bring
forth a statement—is justified only if the meaning of the
work transcends them. I would like my personal mark to have
a clarity and directness like the tracks of the jackrabbit in the
spring snow that say, "Yes, I have been here."*

Henry J. Drexler

Born in Norwich, New York, 1947. Received B.A. 1969 from Cornell University, Ithaca, New York. Attended Munson-Williams-Proctor Institute School of Art, Utica, New York, 1977–78. Has participated in New York State in numerous state and regional group juried exhibitions and in 1980 had one-man exhibitions at Guernsey Memorial Library, Norwich,

and New York State Veterans' Home, Oxford. Received People's Choice Award 1978 from Norwich Fine Arts Guild; was awarded Best in Class 1979 and 1980, and Best in Show 1980 at "Sherburne Art Show," Pennsylvania. Was president of Chenango County (New York) Council of the Arts, Inc., 1977–80. Lives in Norwich, New York.

19.
The Bank Building   1979
acrylic on canvas
30 × 36 (76.2 × 91.4)

As a kid growing up in the country on a dairy farm, I dreamed of traveling and moving to the city. However, after going away to school, touring the United States and Europe, and spending time in Chad, Africa, as a Peace Corps Volunteer, I chose to return to the place from which I started. It is a land of rolling hills, winding streams, and dairy farms. It is a place where hard-working people can live in harmony with nature.

Although I still enjoy visiting cities, particularly New York for its museums, I find most urban environments oppressive to my spirit. Living here has definitely influenced my life and my art. The influence is pervasive, better expressed through my art and lifestyle than through words. Through my art I commune with my environment and with nature.

20.
The Chenango at Sherburne 1980
acrylic on canvas
24 × 30 (61 × 76.2)
Lent by Edward J. Lee, Norwich, New York

51

William R. Dunlap

Born in Webster County, Mississippi, 1944. Received B.A. 1967 from Mississippi College, Clinton, and M.F.A. 1969 from University of Mississippi, University. Has participated in numerous one-man and group exhibitions since 1966 and is widely collected. Has appeared as guest artist and lecturer at numerous museums and universities throughout nation. Was assistant professor, Department of Art, Appalachian State University, Boone, North Carolina, 1977–79; and professor of art and director of Special Projects, Memphis State University, Tennessee, 1979–80. Currently devotes full time to art. Lives in Boone.

left panel

I*t would be impossible to live in and not be visibly influenced by the southern Appalachian mountains. The light, landscape, and weather come together in an unusual fashion here. These are the oldest mountains in this hemisphere, in the world some think. They're all worn down now. Time has left the ridges gracefully curved with soft contours and sinuous lines. As to colors—well, the Blue Ridge is aptly named. Principles of atmospheric perspective are illustrated daily, and nowhere in the South are the seasonal changes more drastic.*

I've come to all this in the past ten years. I was born in northern Mississippi, in those red clay hills that fan out just at the southeastern-most base of the last rise in the ground that could be claimed as part of the Appalachian range. The Natchez Trace, a game trail for the French, Scottish, and Irish settlers on their way south, ran through my home town. It's now a National Park, as is the Blue Ridge Parkway, which follows the ancient Appalachian Trail, used also in its turn by some of the same game, and by Indian, immigrant, and government road builders. I've lived and worked for the past ten years on the apron of this ridge-running highway, near Blowing Rock, North Carolina.

All this might seem insignificant except that my work is all about the landscape that flanks these two officially converted old roads. As a member of that postwar generation set free by (if not conceived in the back seat of) the automobile, and destined now to buy the last gallons of gasoline to drive the last internally combusted mile, and to ease to a final stop on some dismal interstate late one night, I've seen the landscape between New Orleans and New York become a peripheral blur—something glanced at out the window at high speed, a unique perspective—and one that makes the pursuit of absolute clarity more difficult, but no less rewarding.

21.
Early Light—Fogbound I and II   1980
oil and acrylic on panel
diptych: each panel 18 × 79 (45.7 × 200.6)
Lent by Fisher Brothers and Prudential Insurance Company of America, New York, New York

right panel

detail, right panel

Charles J. Eldred

Born in Binghamton, New York, 1938. Received B.A. 1960 from Harpur College, State University of New York at Binghamton. Has participated in numerous exhibitions, including one-man show 1980 at Roberson Center for The Arts and Sciences, Binghamton. Since 1962 has been associate professor of art, State University of New York at Binghamton.

I make things out of parts, attempting to evolve through successive generations of objects and private images a whole that is not only greater than the sum of its parts, but entirely unpredictable from them. They are small sculptures toward a personal millennium, ancient sculptures of the present from the remnants of a past civilization, all made here in the Valley of the Shadow of Opportunity with its hills and rivers, its seasons, smokestacks, green domes, gold domes, fittings, fixtures, and its daily production of small, quietly bizzare visual events and happenstances. They are made by hand, with a deceptive whimsicality and relentless sense of nonsense, to be bright devices for a medieval mid-America in the Gray Ages.

One simply makes things—a basic human activity almost from the beginning. The making is the experience of the artist. Experience is the next best thing to being there.

The experience consists, in part, of a world of images which are suggested, felt, recalled, conjured up, shuffled and matched, which can be thought about only when one works with one's hands.

I am fascinated with the relationships between two and three dimensions, the ordinary physical dimensions of everyday experience, the paradoxes involved in the representation of the

22.
Aviary 1975
pen and ink on paper
30 × 22 (76.2 × 55.9)
(opposite, left)

24.
Terrarium 1973
pen and ink on paper
30 × 22 (76.2 × 55.9)
(opposite, right)

23.
Centaur 1977
iron
7 × 7 × 2 (17.8 × 17.8 × 5.1)
Lent by Jewell and Robert Hoogstoel,
Toledo, Ohio

three dimensional on a two-dimensional surface, and the range and variety of results produced by the continuing attempt. In the process, one is occasionally rewarded by a glimpse into the riddle of how the mind imagines, forms, reforms, and remembers and invents images. Working is a variety of thinking, making is an access to knowing—a game without rules for one player. For the most part, one hopes to fuse disparate, dissimilar pieces into a single configuration that continues to trigger varied responses in the mind.

The drawings and sculptures are made in the same manner; each is assembled from carefully fitted pieces. The drawings tend to be technological structures imposed on biological, natural structures. The sculptures are the opposite—natural, biological forms made from or superimposed on metal, mechanical ones.

Each drawing is part of a larger series and is composed of many small drawings fitted together into a single abstract configuration on a single paper. They are synthesized from many sources—some are drawn directly from life or still life. Some are invented, others evolved through the making of marks, fragments of photographs, engravings, and from a long series of silverpoint drawings made to function as information and parts for the pen-and-ink drawings.

The sculptures deal in contradictions, the putting together of things that don't go together. They are made directly with very simple tools—drills, hacksaws, files, sandpaper, a manually operated drill press, a small grinding tool. Although the parts are cast or machined originally by one industrial process or another, I do no casting or welding or brazing or forging. The pieces are all found, or made from brass plate or stock, carved, wrought, cut up, cut down, cut off, hammered, re-shaped, fitted and fastened together by mechanical means— pinned, wedged, or bolted with tapped holes and threaded rod. The work is done by hand, including polishing. Finding and fitting is the process. Losing the individual parts by fusing them into a whole is the purpose, working and re-working them until it is hardly possible to tell what is found and what is made, until by a process of recognition, it looks as it should—until it becomes not art, but something real, anonymous.

Excerpted from *Charles Eldred: Sculpture and Drawing* (Binghamton, New York: Roberson Center for The Arts and Sciences, 1980). Reprinted by permission of Roberson Center for The Arts and Sciences.

Charles J. Eldred

25.
Winter Camera   1980–81
brass and bronze
31 × 36 × 17½ (78.7 × 91.4 × 44.5)

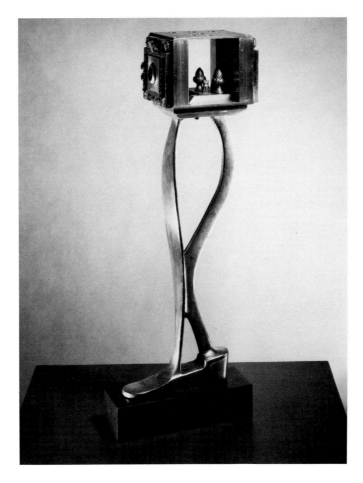

26.
Garden   1979
brass
24 × 5 × 9 (61 × 12.7 × 22.9)

Kenneth W. Evett

Born in Loveland, Colorado, 1913. Received B.A. 1935 from Colorado State College (now University of Northern Colorado), Greeley; studied 1936–39 at Colorado Springs Fine Art Center; and received M.A. 1939 from Colorado College, Colorado Springs. Won Yaddo Fellowships, Saratoga Springs, New York, 1954 and 1959. Taught studio art and art history, Salem Academy and College, Winston-Salem, North Carolina, 1945–46. Served as director of Kendall Foundation, Hot Springs, Virginia, 1947–48. Was freelance art critic for *The New Republic*, 1972–77. Has had group and one-man exhibitions at, among others, Whitney Museum of American Art, New York City; Corcoran Gallery of Art, Washington, D.C.; and Palace of the Legion of Honor, San Francisco, California. Work is in collections of Amon Carter Museum of Western Art, Fort Worth, Texas; Joslyn Museum, Omaha, Nebraska; Munson-Williams-Proctor Museum, Utica, New York; and The Newark Museum, New Jersey. Since 1948 has been on faculty of College of Architecture, Art, and Planning, Cornell University, Ithaca, New York; was chairman of Department of Fine Art, 1974–77; is now professor emeritus.

27.
Portrait of Sibylle Ungers 1979
oil on canvas
38 × 24 (96.5 × 61)
Lent by Kraushaar Galleries, New York, New York

Although I am a firm believer in the theory that geography and climate have a strong influence on an artist's vision, I am not sure in my own case whether my early formative years in the clean air and white light of Colorado, or my mature life in the mists and muted tones of upstate New York have been more decisive. Wherever I have painted, my work has been profoundly affected by the forms and colors of the environment.

Nevertheless, esthetic and formal concerns are also important, and in those matters my attitudes have been influenced by the international perceptions and interests of my colleagues and by my own frequent expeditions to study the great figurative art of the Mediterranean region.

Steve Ferguson

Born in Princeton, Indiana, 1946. Received B.A. 1968 from Eastern Kentucky University, Richmond, Kentucky, and M.A. 1971 from Appalachian State University, Boone, North Carolina. Did production graphics 1974–80 for Appalachian State University and was guest speaker at its Watauga College (Boone) in 1979. Since 1977 has exhibited locally in numerous group and one-man exhibitions; cofounded "Will the Real Gallery Please Stand Up!" in Boone, 1979. Currently teaches Instructional Graphics at Appalachian State University.

28.
Night Fishing 1979
ink and watercolor on paper
11 × 15 (27.9 × 38.1)

*The light in these mountains is
truly a mystical experience*

*Every year my demeanor ebbs
and flows with the shadows*

*Every fall my rebirth and strengthening;
preparation for winter*

*The chopping of wood
as the mountains become
dragon backs at rest   the sound of nothing*

*The deep deep black
the white bright light*

*Actually being awakened by the
moon's glow in late November*

*The ground smell in spring
at Lowell's*

*the damp birds
talking amongst themselves*

the plowing, the rare horse

*We settlers in recent decade band
together much like the first pioneers
after the Cherokee
we around our cooperatives
they around their churches*

*The feeling for community is strong
here, arts and crafts traditional
and my sense of accomplishment
linked forever to my friends' response*

*The remoteness and individuality
enhanced by the secret valleys
and chambers: homes of generations
of survivalists who can make
anything from wood and wire*

*My work: a contribution to
my neighbors, a confirmation
of myself,*

*a testament to the uniqueness and courage
to renew of all these people*

Each piece different, each person

different, each moment different

Howard Finster

29.
Cat   1979
enamel on wood
17½ × 25½ (44.5 × 64.8)
Lent by Clune Walsh, Detroit, Michigan

Howard Finster

Born in Valley Head, Alabama, 1916. Became preacher at sixteen; has been minister of eight churches. First began to paint in 1976. Has exhibited widely in both group and one-man exhibitions, including "Trans-mitters: The Isolate Artist in America," Philadelphia College of Art, Pennsylvania, 1981. Has lectured frequently and has led many workshops throughout the country. Recently retired from preaching and lives in Summerville, Georgia.

30.
He Could Not Be Hid   1977
tractor paint on fiberboard
30½ × 17¼ (77.5 × 43.8)
Lent by American Folklife Center, Library of Congress, Washington, D.C.

Frank Fleming

Born in Bear Creek, Alabama, 1940. Studied 1958–62 at Florence State College, Alabama; received M.A. 1969 and M.F.A. 1973 from University of Alabama, Birmingham. Has had one-man exhibitions at, among others, Birmingham Museum of Art, 1974; University of Montevallo Art Gallery, Alabama, 1978; Hunter Museum of Art, Chattanooga, Tennessee, 1980. Group exhibitions include "Southern Realism," Mississippi Museum of Art, Jackson, 1979–80; and "American Porcelain: New Expressions in an Ancient Art," Renwick Gallery, National Museum of American Art, Smithsonian Institution, Washington, D.C., 1980–81. Has received many purchase awards and prizes for his work.

31.
A Dog's Painful Search for Knowledge   1980
figure 12
porcelain
17 × 36 × 22   (43.2 × 91.4 × 55.9)
Lent by Myron Friedman, Shawnee Mission, Kansas

Growing up in the backwoods of Alabama, where families—ours in particular—tend to be self-sufficient in many ways, has given me an interesting perception concerning humans and their association with nature. Certain parts of my imagery and subject matter come from my imagination as a child; I was afraid of the dark because I feared that living rhinos and other large animals would charge out of the woods at me. Then, on the other hand, there exists a peaceful quality concerning my subject matter of animals because, being "backward" (a term my family used to refer to our backwoods environment) we, especially me, trusted animals more than humans. We tilled the land with animals and derived our food source from them, and in general animals became our neighbors. My furniture theme came from our having been extremely poor. We had straightback chairs during most of my youth and I dreamed of nice sofas and chairs. We finally acquired enough money to buy a "country modern" living-room suite that we kept covered with feedsack sheets, which were removed on Sunday when we wore our "Sunday clothes." Our more sacred thoughts came from nature, because there was great evidence of its power, which was repeated season after season. Families that lived close to the land like we did learned to respect and look for the "signs" of nature in our day-to-day existence. Today these signs are still an important aspect of myself and my sculpture.

Jean Thickens Francis

Born in Laurel, Mississippi, 1943. Studied 1961–63 at Millsaps College, Jackson, Mississippi; received B.F.A. 1963 from Memphis Academy of Arts, Tennessee. Taught sculpture at Memphis Academy of Arts, summer 1974. Taught art under National Endowment for the Arts program, "Artists in the Schools," in city schools, Jackson, 1976. Taught graphic art at Penland School of Crafts, North Carolina, 1978. Has exhibited widely throughout South in group and one-woman exhibitions, as well as in two-person exhibitions with husband Ke Francis, Jr. Has received numerous awards, including Grand Prize at "Mississippi Artists Competitive Exhibition," Mississippi Art Association, Jackson, 1976; and First Prize for mixed media, "Art Annual One," Tulsa, Oklahoma, 1980. Shares studio with husband in Tupelo, Mississippi.

32.
Memories of a Moth   1980
collage: handmade paper
24½ × 20 × 4 (62.2 × 51 × 10.2)
Lent by Dr. Thomas Tyra, Cullowhee, North Carolina

Memories of a Moth is made of a stack of watercolored and/or printed handmade papers with bookbinding paper that reminds me of old wallpapers found in many southern homes. The watercolored print of a moth and silk string binding the papers together are symbols of the moth's "memories" of all the places it has been in its small lifetime. This collage was made for a friend in Tupelo who always created warm, beautiful surroundings—ones in which I felt at home, as if they carried inside this one house all the places one has ever loved, all the stages one has lived through, all the memories one has acquired, brought together in one space and time.

Ten years ago my husband Ke, our daughter Kerry, and I moved into a family fishing cabin in the woods of northeast Mississippi. We found that when one lives in the country, communication is much more intuitive: mental telepathy has become for us a workable alternative to a telephone. The images, visions, and dreams that we would so quickly share in a city must wait until a letter can be written. A gift of pecans, jams, and pickles must be wrapped very carefully and sent by mail.

My work has grown out of this physical isolation and lag in normal communication. From every direction I began to feel the subtle messages that are always being sent. The messages I send to those far away are ones of a peaceful dawn, a quiet

moment in still, wet woods, or the quality and patterns of light.

The tiny details or wild expanses of nature are the fabrics that I dye, tear, and pour into paper. The moments that I wish to share become the porcelain stamps, letters, and gifts. The photoetchings are glimpses of friends and family and places loved as memory gives them back to us in her strange collaged fashion. The threads of silk or dyed cords are used as symbols of "ties," bonds that revitalize and reinforce like the rain. Everything in these collages relates to what is most real to me— our human spirit and its ties (with nature and each other) and the unbelievable variations with which we use them, communicate them, and celebrate them.

33.
Rainbow Fallout 1980
* figure 10 (color)
collage: handmade paper with printed details
40 × 28 (101.6 × 71.1)

This collage is made of sheets of different kinds of handmade paper. The biggest sheet is made from 100 percent rag papers and papers from old prints and watercolors, with chips of favorite old shirts that encompass a lifetime. It is reminiscent of our southern patchwork quilts made of everyone's old clothes. It also reminds me of being *in* a rainbow—all the particles of lighted droplets of color. The grassy-green/purple piece is made of corn shucks and thistle, with a little oriental rice paper to hold it together better. The stack of tiny sheets are all handmade 100 percent rag papers, some with silk threads, others printed. The images are printed, watercolor, and photoetched images—tiny moments of wild flowers. "Fallout" to me is what is left *after* an experience. *Rainbow Fallout* is what is left after experiencing a rainbow!

34.
Southern Summer Gift 1980
collage: handmade paper with porcelain
18 × 18 × 1½ (45.7 × 45.7 × 3.8)

Southern Summer Gift is a porcelain image of a pecan sprout. The next layer is hand-poured paper with the pecan-sprig image stamped as a border. The largest sheet of handmade paper has in four corners embroidered leaves and flowers from some pillowcases of Ke's eighty-four-year-old grandmother. She does beautiful handwork. I couldn't tear her work to shreds to make paper out of it, so I used it as it was in the paper. The trees are a gift to anyone in the South during our horribly hot summers. In particular, the giant pecan trees in the backyard of Ke's grandparents make the coolest spot in town. Those tiny pecan sprouts are a *real* gift!

Ke Francis, Jr.

Born in Memphis, Tennessee, 1945. Studied at Mississippi State University, Starkville; Memphis State University, Tennessee; and Cape School of Art, Provincetown, Massachusetts. Received B.F.A. 1969 from Cleveland Institute of Art, Ohio. Taught at Memphis Academy of Arts, Tennessee, summer 1973; and Penland School of Crafts, North Carolina, 1978–79. Led clay sculpture workshop at Hepworth-Galet Pipe Factory, Andenne, Belgium, 1979. Has been included in numerous juried, group, and one-man exhibitions, and has also had two-person exhibitions with wife Jean Thickens Francis. Has received numerous awards, including Best in Show, "Fourth Mississippi-Alabama Bi-State," Meridian Museum of Art, Mississippi, 1977. Shares studio with wife in Tupelo, Mississippi.

35.
Tupelo Tornado Relic   1981
construction: steel, wood, tin, and paper
44 × 30 × 8 (11.8 × 76.2 × 20.3)

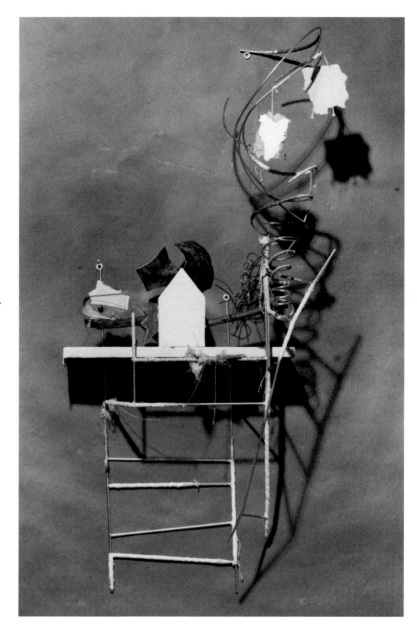

Like most artists working in rural areas today, I work with a well-educated and more sophisticated visual vocabulary than most of my regional predecessors. I received an art-school education and am well traveled. I am familiar with current art trends and with work being done in the cities of this country (New York, Chicago, Los Angeles, etc.). Although I am not interested in faking naïveté, there is something of the primitive in my work. I think primitive cultures had a way of dealing with the whole man (the dark side as well as the light side). Art for them was a functional process. It created its own mythology, sustained its culture's important values, and grew and changed as it incorporated new stories from its culture. I think artists who have chosen to represent the values of their people (no matter where they are located physically) rep-resent a new thrust in American art. It may be that in our short history we have covered the surface of our artistic concerns to our satisfaction and that some real depth needs to be cut in our cultural topography. It is going to require a new and expansive myth. It is going to require a link with the land and some kind of bridge between folk history (folk tales, legends, etc.) and the formal elements and surface developments of current American art.

I have been living and working in Mississippi for ten years. Four generations of my family live within fifteen miles of one another. The concerns I spoke of are my artistic concerns and I sense a growing company of artists out there who share them.

Thomas J. Golya

37.
Suckerhead 1980
wood, spray and brush enamel
7 × 37 (17.8 × 94)

Born in Akron, Ohio 1940. Received
B.F.A. 1965 from Kent State University,
Ohio, and M.F.A. 1967 from Ohio University, Athens. Taught at University of
Maine at Augusta, 1967–74 and State University of New York at Fredonia, 1974–75.
Was artist in residence, Chautauqua
County (New York) Association for the
Arts, Dunkirk, 1978–79. Since 1974 has
exhibited in numerous one-man and group
exhibitions. Lives in Forestville, New
York.

*Having lived in southern Ohio and northern Pennsylvania,
and now in northwestern New York, all segments of Appalachia, I find the rural environment has made a strong impression on me and on my work. I have found the people of rural
Appalachia to be determined and uniquely self-sufficient, a
people whose pride is closely related to the history, folklore,*

Thomas J. Golya

Robert A. Gough

and surrounding environment of the region. The rural environment allows me to collect the materials I use in my work, such as wood, stone, animal skeletons, and the like. The folklore of the area titillates my imagination, and the history, such as that of the Indian Mound Builders of southern Ohio or of the once powerful and structured Seneca Nation of New York, holds an appeal and has had an influence on my work. In addition, the color variations I use are related to the cycles and gyrations of Appalachian nature.

Born in Quebec City, Canada, 1931. Studied 1949–53 at American Academy of Art, Chicago. Has been included in exhibitions at The Art Institute of Chicago, Illinois; Pennsylvania Academy of The Fine Arts, Philadelphia; Walker Art Center, Minneapolis, Minnesota; and Oklahoma Art Center, Oklahoma City. Has received Henry Ward Ranger Prize from National Academy of Design, New York City, and Purchase Prize from The Butler Institute of American Art, Youngstown, Ohio. Lives in Chillicothe, Ohio.

36.
Happiness/Madness Landscape Segment (An Allegory)   1979
figure 11
steel rod, glass, copper plate, wood,
fungus, and paint
77 × 20 × 56 (195.6 × 50.8 × 142.2)

38.
Winter Store   1980
oil on canvas
12 × 16 (30.5 × 40.6)
Lent by Mary and Cy Rutledge, Chillicothe, Ohio

39.
Summer Opening   1979
oil on panel
12 × 16 (30.5 × 40.6)
Lent by Mr. and Mrs. John Haynes
Barnhart, Chillicothe, Ohio

There are various reasons why I have chosen not only to live in this area of southern Ohio, but also to have it serve as the main subject matter of my work. The most essential reason is that I consider it "home." Although I was not born in Chilli-cothe and have lived elsewhere, I resided in this community during the formative years of growing up. The time that I spent away from it only confirmed my emotional involvement with this particular part of Appalachia. There would always be those times when the feel of a day would put me in mind of something I had experienced in Ross County, Ohio.

As one of the earliest settlements in Ohio, Chillicothe is in a region rooted in tradition and history. This enhances the enjoyment and inspiration I gain from the rich tradition of landscape painting. Moreover, since this is largely an agricultural area, eternal themes are always evident—the cyclical changes of the seasons, the logic and order contained in nature, the relationship of man and woman to the land.

Through the effects of glaciers centuries before, there is a wide variety of terrain here, and there are moments when prevailing weather conditions lend a spectacular and dramatic intensity to various vistas, but for the most part the region has a quiet, subtle, understated beauty. Perhaps this is what gives it its seemingly universal feeling of familiarity.

Lowell Hayes

Born in Johnson County, Tennessee, 1936.
Received B.A. 1958 from Lynchburg College, Virginia, and B.D. 1965 from Divinity School of the University of Chicago, Illinois. Author of *Lowell's Illustrated Shelter Thinkbook*, privately published in 1972. Since 1974 has been instructor at Watauga College, Appalachian State University, Boone, North Carolina. Has exhibited locally.

front view

I *don't remember, if I ever knew, what precise event is considered the shot that opened World War II, but it may as well have occurred—like the nation's first fiddlers' convention—at Mountain City, Tennessee, for it blew away a whole culture right here in my own hills, in my own lifetime. Consequently, much of my growing up and learning energy were occupied with acculturation. Like an immigrant, I had to be naturalized in order to find a new place in the new culture, with the difference that I did not immigrate; the new culture came, rather, to my homeland.*

When I was a child, my grandparents and my parents (though my mother started early to modify her speech) used a very pure southern-Appalachian dialect, which to outlanders sounded like a foreign language. It was an emotive, musical speech that harkened back to the sixteenth century; governed by its own conventions, it was capable of superb expression. Now "Gran'paw," pushing ninety, sounds like Walter Cronkite.

I used to sneak up to my "Gran'maw's" attic and play with her quilt pieces. Those colorful bits of fabric, I perceived, were both very important and very personal to her. She was my buddy. She was so important to me that to investigate the sorted combinations of colors, textures, patterns, and shapes was like entering into her very being and partaking of her essential reality. I was her favorite, her adored. I and I alone was permitted, even encouraged, to make suggestions for new combinations as I helped her sort through the pieces. The attic was actually off-bounds to unsupervised young'uns, but I always went up when she did. She, of course, pretended not to

notice that I often went without her, and I understood that to mean that she trusted me in a special way because of the precious knowledge that we shared up there. The great mainstream culture, in its generosity, created the TVA to raise its literal tide above the attic's tin skin. Not long after I learned to spell aesthetic with an "a," my grandmother died. At fifty, the hills had used her up. Her tiny, delicate frame just broke like the wing of a little blue butterfly, and she was gone.

There was another grandmother, who, legend has it, took me in her arms and called me her little preacher, thus setting into motion by her matriarchal authority the spiral that was to take me through the church to the world of the times and spaces beyond the hills.

My parents prospered as enthusiastic participants in the exciting new (to them) culture of Progress, escaping the depression and reveling in its invincibility. I was the first from either side of the family to go to college. I traveled, went to seminary, gorged myself to the point of overindulgence at the world's cultural banquet. I was a social activist, an antiarchitect, a schoolteacher, a minister, a creator of institutions, a corporation president. Like any other hillbilly in Chicago or Pittsburgh, I was there because what I thought I wanted could not be found at home. Like any other hillbilly who comes home, I realized, eventually, that what I really wanted was what I could find at home.

Out of what I did find here, I make expressions of what I find here. My daily life is filled with marvelous encounters with the intimate time-event details of the natural setting

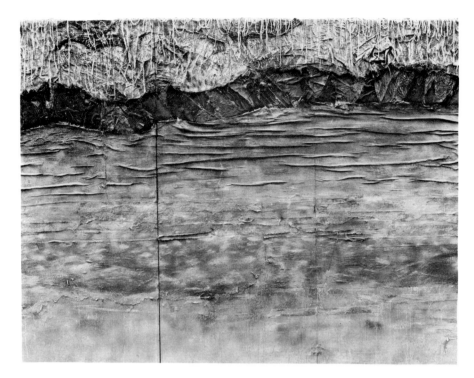

back view

made intensely available by the sensitivity of my matriarchs and my own years of longing absence. The leftovers of our wasteful new society, more than sufficient in light of the ingenuity required of my patriarchs, are resources for shaping my offertories and the basics of a living: food, shelter, aesthetics. It's pretty damn spooky when you realize that I'm still up in the attic (my studio is at the top of my house) sorting bits of colored fabrics; but there's a great deal more to it than that. Here in my hills I also find a free, happy community of poets, artists, scholars, homesteaders, aesthetes, clowns, shamans; spiritual, principled, generous, sophisticated, loving people.

I have a sense that there is a power available to me here, and to many others who wish to pursue aesthetic or spiritual matters. I don't think this power is available to the self-seeking, the exploitative, or the slick; not here. So, far from using me up (I will soon be as old as Gran'maw when she died), these mountains daily recreate and nurture me as no other place or people I can find.

I did not come back here to look for what is no more. I don't like "barn paintings," craft fairs, or the exploitation of nostalgia. I love Mozart, David Del Tredici, Doc Watson, Japanese aesthetics, cornbread and beans, latter-day flower children, rhododendron groves, Steve Ferguson's paintings, bold relief in the geography, lots of clean water, black gospel, the woods in winter, Jay Wentworth's poems, and my annual gallery party. I am a christian (small "c") atheist of the everyday (Zen) mind. I am a contemporary Appalachian.

40.
A T.V.A. Commonplace   1980
figure 1 (color)
mixed fabrics and paints on hinged
hollow-core birch doors
80 × 108 × 3 (203.2 × 274.3 × 7.6)

A T.V.A. Commonplace has four sides, all of which are equally important and intimately interconnected, so that each is incomplete without the other three. Two large sides, representing my birthplace before and after it was covered by Watauga Lake, are completed by the exposed ends or edges of the panels on which are the legends

In the Greater Tennessee Valley the T.V.A. had done much to eradicate rural poverty.
and
What was, in 1936, the site of the town of Butler, Tennessee, is now covered by a T.V.A. Commonplace known as Watauga Lake; as is the V.E. Lipford place nearby, where I was born that year.

The style of the whole piece is my own invention and is a technical summary of all that has gone before.

One side shows the farm as I remember it from age eleven, when last I saw it. I did not use photographs because I wanted to depend upon that residual, emotional impression. My grandfather, V.E. Lipford, and other members of the family assure me that it is quite accurate except for certain "editorial" arbitrations that I made for reasons of composition and overall emotional and artistic harmony. I have used shiny material for emotional emphasis on an otherwise soft, matte, low-intensity coloration.

On the obverse side the same scene is presented as if seen through the format, now covered by the lake, the raw red clay, purple shale bank above the water's edge providing the only real pictorial motif. The trees in the woods at the top of the design are actually the same as those on the other side; the acrylic-filled fibres of which they are made continue right over the top of

Lowell Hayes

Lonnie B. Holley

the panels to either side. The large boulder in the bank is seen in the steep hillside pasture overpanel. And, as if deep under the water, there are subtle, shiny ghosts of the farmhouse and dependencies. The general feeling of the "farm side" is one of arresting impressionistic realism, while that of the "lake side" is nearly abstract expressionist or perhaps oriental in design, but definitely à la contemporary. So that, while the whole is locked together by a whole series of devices, the drastic contrast is what creates the shocking recognition of the real. It is the same place. I am the same person. It is no more the place it was than I am the person I was.

Born in Birmingham, Alabama, 1950. Attended public schools in Birmingham. Has exhibited in Birmingham at Jefferson State College, there receiving award from Afro-American Society, 1981; and at Sixth Avenue Baptist Church. Currently serves as volunteer sculpture teacher at local schools and colleges. Lives in Birmingham.

I *want to take the time out to say thank you for your time that you gave to help me. I have not been into art but eight months. I asked God to give me something so that I may go to the top in life and he did, and you have a part in it. I got to the fourth grade in school. My mother had twenty-seven kids and I am the seventh, but things have been bad for me all my life. So I asked God to help me and he did. Thank you all, and may God be for you all.*

41.
Baby Being Born 1979–80
sandstone
18 × 15 × 6 (45.7 × 38.1 × 15.2)

42.
Time 1979–80
sandstone
11 × 28 × 6 (27.9 × 71.1 × 15.2)

Vernon F. Howell

Born in Huntington, West Virginia, 1935. Received B.A. 1960 from Marshall University, Huntington, West Virginia, and M.A. 1967 from George Washington University, Washington, D.C. Taught part time at Marshall University, 1968–72; and The Huntington Galleries, Inc., West Virginia, 1970. Has won awards for his work and is represented in The Huntington Galleries, Inc. Since 1961 has been high school art instructor. Lives in Barboursville, West Virginia.

43.
Tools and Cabinet   1980
acrylic on masonite
32 × 48 (81.3 × 121.9)

My first exposure to contemporary art was in the early '50s, my freshman year at Syracuse University. This was quite a change compared to my first eighteen years of living in Huntington, West Virginia. But since then, through my formal training and teaching, all the trends of art have become an integral part of my development although I have continued to live in West Virginia. During the past few years, I have felt a need to reflect in my work to a greater degree a closer association between my art and my experiences drawn from the area where I live and intend to live the rest of my life.

In the last series of paintings, I have utilized the camera, which is my companion in many of my outdoor activities (hunting, hiking, fishing, and camping). After selecting the subject, I shoot ten to fifty photographs. By developing and processing my own films, I can control the final print to emphasize what seems important. The process I use most is a Kodalith print in which I can eliminate the intermediate tones and add emphasis to parts of the composition. The color selection of the paintings involves trial combinations, sometimes as many as thirty. I apply the transparent underpainting of acrylics with sponges and/or rollers. The opaque paint is applied by brush.

Victor Huggins

44.
Near Salem   1975
cover
acrylic on canvas
61 × 49 (154.9 × 124.5)
Lent by Roanoke Museum of Fine Arts,
Roanoke, Virginia

73

Victor Huggins

Born in Chapel Hill, North Carolina, 1936. Received B.A. 1962 and M.A.C.A. 1966 from University of North Carolina at Chapel Hill. Has participated in one-man and group exhibitions throughout eastern United States. Received Virginia Museum Fellowship, 1973. Has received numerous awards for painting, most recently at The Southeastern Center for Contemporary Art, Winston-Salem, North Carolina, 1977. Is represented in private and public collections throughout nation. Currently is professor and head, Department of Art, College of Arts and Sciences, Virginia Polytechnic and State University, Blacksburg, Virginia.

Having started a highly successful career as an abstract painter, I moved to the Appalachian Mountains in 1969 to join the art faculty at Virginia Tech in Blacksburg. Soon after my first New York one-man show of color abstractions at the Bertha Schaefer Gallery in 1970, I found that the serene beauty and ethereal nature of the surrounding mountains began to have a strong influence on my work. By 1973 I had completed my first series of mountainscapes, which were exhibited at The Southeastern Center for Contemporary Art in Winston-Salem. During this year I took a yearlong leave to live and work in New York City, where I completed over thirty major landscape paintings and a large number of drawings and prints.

After living in Blacksburg for three years, surrounded by the beauty and calm force of the Appalachian Mountains, I found that I could no longer resist their temptation; they thrust their way, as relentlessly as they came from the earth, into my consciousness and onto my canvas. Oh, those omnific, undulating, sensuous forms can be whatever they want to be:

> frozen — fleeting
> opaque — transparent
> concrete — nebulous
> positive — negative
> heavy — light
> crisp — atmospheric
> singular — plural
> intense — subdued
> ostentatious — subtle
> strong - fragile
> regular — random

It is their metamorphic, ephemeral nature that attracts my attention; it is their atmospheric condition that I so admire. When it is their moment to be

calm	still	cool
serene	quiet	placid
peaceful	tranquil	composed
collected	undisturbed	unruffled
unperturbable	self-possessed	dispassionate
	and	
	unpredictable	

this is their time I want others to feel and see.

While my paintings of mountains are realistic, they represent abstractions—my ideals.

74

Angelo Ippolito

Born in San Arsenio, Italy, 1922. Studied 1946 at Ozenfant School of Fine Arts, New York City; 1948 at Brooklyn Museum Art School, Brooklyn, New York; and 1949 at Instituto Meschini, Rome, Italy. Received Fulbright Fellowship, Florence, Italy, 1959; Ford Foundation artist-in-residence grant, 1965; and Tiffany Foundation grant, 1979. Has exhibited internationally in numerous one-man and group exhibitions. Is represented in Whitney Museum of American Art, New York City; The Phillips Collection, Washington, D.C.; The Museum of Modern Art, New York City; and many other collections. Has taught at many colleges and universities throughout nation. Since 1971 has been professor of art, State University of New York at Binghamton.

45.
Winter Landscape   1977–78
figure 5 (color)
oil on canvas
77 × 100 (195.6 × 254)
Lent by Borgenicht Gallery, New York, New York

Not until my last trip to Italy did I realize why I was so attracted to the landscape of the Binghamton area of New York State. In 1973 I took my eleven-year-old son Jon to Europe, a combination sentimental journey and grand tour. One of the places we visited was the valley of Teggiano in the Campania region of southern Italy. On the foot of one of the mountains in the valley is San Arsenio, the place in which I was born.

The mountains there are more dramatic, the ancient towns smaller, the Tanagro River not so large as the Susquehanna, but the light and the configuration of the landscape are quite similar in feeling. Perhaps the southern tier of New York State is softer, with more green in summer and more white in winter, but the rocky land is just as hard to farm. The light in the Binghamton landscape is full of drama, an ever-changing softness, a clean softness. The countryside still maintains a rural quality, especially in Pennsylvania close by.

My paintings have always been about landscape, even the still lifes—not the kind of landscape you see, but the one you feel. Painting has been for me the surrender of self and the joining with nature.

Ron Isaacs

Born in Cincinnati, Ohio, 1941. Received
B.A. 1963 from Berea College, Kentucky,
and M.F.A. 1965 from Indiana University,
Bloomington. Won Woodrow Wilson Fel-
lowship, 1963. Taught in Kentucky at Sue
Bennett College, London, 1965–69, and at
Union College, Barboursville, summer
1968. Has been included in numerous
group exhibitions, including "The Animal
Image: Contemporary Objects and the
Beast," Renwick Gallery of the National
Museum of American Art, Smithsonian
Institution, Washington, D.C.; and "The
Reality of Illusion," traveling exhibition
that opened 1979 at The Denver Art Mu-
seum, Colorado. Has had one-man exhibi-
tions at, among others, World Heritage
Museum, University of Illinois at
Champaign-Urbana, 1978; and at Monique
Knowlton Gallery, New York City, 1977,
1978, and 1980. Has won numerous pur-
chase and merit awards. Since 1967 has
taught at Eastern Kentucky University,
Richmond, and is currently professor of
art there.

46.
Black Dress with Scissors   1978
*figure 14
construction: acrylic on birch plywood
46 × 25½ × 2½ (116.8 × 64.8 × 6.3)
Lent by Gayle and Andrew Camden, Detroit, Michigan; courtesy of Monique
Knowlton Gallery, New York, New York

47.
Jabot   1980
construction: acrylic on birch plywood
39 × 59 × 7¾ (99 × 149.9 × 19.7)
Lent by Monique Knowlton Gallery, New
York, New York

I stress formal considerations and visual relationships over
other kinds of content in my work, but I also choose subject
matter for complex reasons having to do with past associations. These are largely beyond my full understanding. The
leaves and sticks from Kentucky woods that appear frequently
in my pieces are the most obvious reference to my immediate
environment, but the use of antique clothing as imagery may
have much to do with the "feel" of the country and the continued life of its past in its present.

A search for relationships can easily be pushed too far, but
the fact remains that much of my personality was formed by
parents who were from eastern Kentucky; moreover, my ado-
lescence, college years, and professional life to date have been
spent here. The background and environment for so much of
my life must have influenced me—and therefore my work.

Judy V. Jones

Born in Winston-Salem, North Carolina, 1949. Received B.F.A. 1972 and M.F.A. 1976 from University of Georgia, Athens. Exhibited at The Southeastern Center for Contemporary Art, 1980, and The Mint Museum of Art, Charlotte, North Carolina, 1981. Since 1976 has been assistant professor of art, Converse College, Spartanburg, South Carolina.

This is a difficult question to answer specifically. I am sure that because I have lived my entire life—so far—in Appalachia that I have been influenced by this region in one way or another. I feel that I make very personal art. My work is part of my life and the people that inhabit it, and many of these people live and work in this region. In this sense Appalachia means a great deal to me. On the other hand, I have traveled widely and have tried not to let living in this region of the country insulate me from contemporary ideas in all parts of the world. We have become such a culture of mass communication and the media that I feel regionalism may be disappearing.

48.
Mellors 1977
intaglio on paper
22½ × 14½ (57.1 × 36.8)
(above)

49.
Once Again 1978
intaglio on paper
23 × 26½ (58.4 × 67.3)

R. Benjamin Jones

Born in Sparrows Point, Maryland, 1936. Received B.A. 1962 from University of Maryland at College Park and M. Div. 1966 from Pittsburgh Theological Seminary, Pennsylvania. Taught art appreciation and basic drawing and painting at Hagerstown Junior College, Maryland,

1980–81. Had one-man exhibition at Hagerstown Junior College, 1975; also exhibited 1971–80 in "Cumberland Valley Juried Exhibition," Washington County Museum of Fine Arts, Hagerstown, there receiving nine awards in ten years.

50.
Jacques' Farm, Cavetown   1979
watercolor on paper
10⅛ × 26⅛ (25.7 × 66.4)
Lent by Mr. and Mrs. George S. Weikart, Jr., Hagerstown, Maryland

In the fifteen years I have lived in Washington County, Maryland, I have been very much aware of the way in which change is taking place. There are farms that have been operating for 200 years, but which won't be around for twenty more. I have become close to these farms, the families on them, and all the pieces and parts of what has been a part of their tradition. What they see simply as the daily work of four generations on this plot of ground, I see with a sense of wonder as a passing way of life. I've been around to record the last gasp of what had been a thriving farm—seventy-five years of cared-for buildings given over to weeds and weather, or to the developer. That kind of thing ought not pass without some sort of comment. I'm trying to make that comment. I look at the great accumulation of simple things on the farm

and see the love and care that got mixed in with the labor. I'm trying to see and record (so that others can see) that mysterious blend of the tough and the gentle that made farming happen in this county. It's not that I want to stop progress; let the houses and businesses come. But before all the gold vinyl siding gets nailed onto the 200-year-old stone walls, I want to make some loving notes. They'll never be just that way again. I'm happy that this country (my part of Appalachia) has enough of its farms to last the rest of my painting life. Living in the midst of the farms has kept me in constant touch with them. Something in what I kept seeing touched a creative place in me. Maybe I would be just as sensitive to the shape and movement of the city, I don't know. But I know it has happened here.

Caryl Jones-Sylvester

Born in Newark, New Jersey, 1943. Received M.F.A. 1973 from Rutgers University, New Brunswick, New Jersey. Is represented in The Newark Museum of Fine Arts, New Jersey. Lives in Cameron Mills, New York.

51.
Suppertime   1981
figure 7
mixed construction
$8 \times 11 \times 2$ feet ($2.4 \times 3.3 \times 0.6$ millimeters)

Like my grandfather, my husband Noel is a junker. Without his help, I could never have made *Suppertime*. Scrap metal that Noel had stockpiled for years forms much of the armature for the piece. A neighbor's dog coop, broken down and reconstructed, became Bev, Al, Wanda, Ronnie, and Dora. Lighting fixtures from a burned-out trailer, antler "racks" considered inferior by the standards of local hunters, crazed linoleum rugs, plastic scraps, and even my paints and brushes have been "donated" by people enthusiastic about *Suppertime*.

The dioramas of *Suppertime* are recessed in the side pieces. They are: 1) the inside of a pop-top camper, night-lighted for card games; 2) Dora's dresser top, which is a kind of iconography: her grandchildren, praying hands, etc., on the wall, a gun rack that serves to hold clothing and, for cosmetics, a rear-view mirror from a Chevy; 3) Bev's trailer, small against the hills, small relative to the springloaded rocking horse of her eight children; 4) the Log Cabin tavern, where you cash your check on payday, have a cool one, listen to tunes, and take two six-packs of Genny out the back door (for the road); 5) "Potatoes and Pigs"—digging the patch and butchering the hog, inseparable; 6) hunting season, the stark hills dotted with the orange Day-Glo of men stalking that eight-point buck.

The crown that *Suppertime* wears is a part of every trailer's dooryard. When all that remains is the cinderblocks used to level a trailer home, the swing set says, "people lived here once."

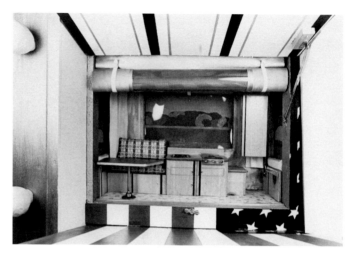

detail

detail

79

Caryl Jones-Sylvester

The whole is equal to the sum of its parts.

Here in upstate New York, much of day-to-day trailer life is documented in decal. Hopes and dreams get glued to one another, and trailers become moving murals. Inside, a couple of fuzzy rollers make personal compositions out of 4′0″ by 8′0″ sheet paneling. Outside, the metal pop-riveted skin celebrates change—change in the season, change in the disposition of the occupants. The jacks and hitch are structural as well as symbolic: *Suppertime* could conceivably pack up and pull out should high water threaten or jamboree call.

Interior space is an acknowledged necessity here when the weather is particularly harsh. But outside is where life is lived: hunting, trapping, and fishing; tending a handful of chickens, a pig or two, and a coon hound; tracking up the "crike" bed; digging the garden patch; tinkering on ancient but workable farm equipment; drawing maple sap and making apple and pear cider (and later, applejack); and chopping wood—days, weeks, months worth of wood to cut.

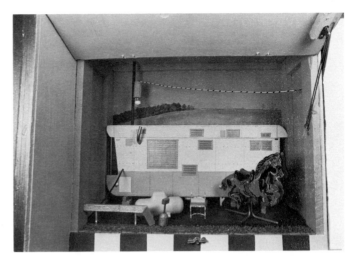

detail

detail

*I*n *Europe my family farmed or worked in the mills. In the United States we farmed rocks in Oneonta, New York, or worked in New Jersey in the thread mills of East Newark, Kearny, Harrison.*

Urban or rural, with little if any schooling (my grandmother often mused, "My education has been sadly neglected") and steeped in "footstomping old-time religion," we were mighty of heart, however "poor of this world" the clan may have been.

My first ten years were spent in the home of my grandfather, who was a junker. I witnessed how someone else's discard, resurrected and repaired, could become new, translated. To me, then is now. At five, I traveled the Bowery with my father. That same summer I visited Oneonta for the first time. And there were no differences. You can see what a cake is made of when it has no icing.

Suppertime is dedicated to the glory of people and places of-

detail

detail

The music of this place is wired and strapped to all things. It is Bob Wills and bluegrass; Tammy, the plaintive "voice of heartbreak"; tambourine and jew's harp; autoharp of the traveling Stonemen; blare of beer joint; good-natured banter or raucous disagreement of working people trying to "make do"; cough of exhausted old engines and roar of motorcycles; and, like an acetate overlay, always, always gospel: walls made of jasper, streets of gold, mansions in the sky. Listen to this music and you can hear God.

Because *Suppertime* is intended to be a microcosm of all of life, it should have something to say to everyone about the various processes we call "living." After all, not long ago Ida Cole stopped by after grange meeting, assayed the project, and declared, "It's understandable, Caryl." And I know Ida knows about "things."

ten disparaged. There is beauty and order in all things; patterns within patterns. All we need do is hear with our ears, see with our eyes.

Among family and friends I am considered a religious fanatic and answer to the names "Halleluja Sylvester" and "Zealot Jones." After I had started Suppertime, *my husband Noel and I had occasion to be in New York City. We walked into the Whitney Museum and I saw a piece by James Hampton called* The Throne, *on loan there from the National Museum of American Art. The spiritual dimension of this work made it alive to me; the impact was so powerful that I started to cry. I came home determined to build and paint my way to the "Glory of God," as Hampton had obviously done with his* Throne. *I knew that my own project must also be "alive" before anyone saw it. All of the information I needed for my purpose was there in my head (with specific information in notebooks), ready to be picked. I waited, listened, and looked, and knew what to do next.*

For me, the microcosm of Suppertime *includes all of life. Most of all, it is about dreams and hope, about coping and prevailing. We all have dreams, each different but all the same. In* Suppertime, *Bev dreams about a new trailer. Like the "super rats" I read about in* National Geographic, *Bev and her family [see fig. 7] will always be. They are tough, they adapt; and they never quit. They know joy often although they may suffer much; because they have their dreams they never lose hope.*

Moses in the wilderness, Romanian gypsies moving east to west, pilgrims crossing the westward sea to a new land, pioneers traveling toward the sunset in covered wagons, contemporary citizens deserting city for suburb and suburb for new homes in sunlit climes, the RV (recreational vehicle) culture of The Long Long Trailer—*moving, moving.*

Life gets built and moves along.

Katherine Kadish

Born in Pittsburgh, Pennsylvania, 1939.
Received B.F.A. 1961 from Carnegie Institute of Technology (now Carnegie-Mellon
University), Pittsburgh, and M.A. from
University of Chicago, Illinois. Taught
1975–80 at State University of New York
at Binghamton, and has held numerous
temporary teaching appointments. Has
participated in major group exhibitions,
among them "Library of Congress Biennial Print Exhibition," 1973, and "Oklahoma Art Center National Exhibition of
Prints and Drawings," 1973 and 1976. Is
the recipient of numerous awards and fellowships. Work is included in New York
State in Munson-Williams-Proctor Institute, Utica, and Roberson Center for The
Arts and Sciences, Binghamton; and is
also included in many other collections.
Lives in Binghamton.

52.
Women in a Garden   1978
pencil on paper
69 × 60 (175.3 × 152.4)

53.
Swimmer Standing   1977
acrylic on paper
33 × 28 (83.8 × 71.1)

M*y work and I essentially grew up in this part of upstate New York. It has affected me in ways I understand and, I am sure, in many ways I do not.*

The first drawings and etchings I made here used the rural landscape of southern New York and northern Pennsylvania: the fields divided by lines of trees and stone walls, the reflecting surfaces of ponds and rivers, the masses of trees and hills. I found artifacts in Pittsburgh and objects and photographs in antique shops and local historical societies that were related to my own family history. I moved into a house in Binghamton of the same era (the 1890s) as the house my grandfather had built in Pittsburgh, where I spent the first nine years of my life. After awhile, however, the connections became more formal in visual terms and had less to do with specific objects.

The real and imaginary gardens of my childhood became the formal gardens and other ordered spaces of the paintings I began in 1978.

Sun, water, shifting light, and the shapes of shadows have always held power for me. The flat gray winters here have made those elements even more precious, and I seek them out in my work. I have often needed to "away" from the familiar and ordinary in situations where work was the only thing to be done in order to take the greatest risks. In recent years I have worked fruitfully in Saratoga Springs and in western Virginia near the Blue Ridge Mountains, but I realize that I always see those landscapes, that color and light, against the constant of this place.

Edward Kellogg

Born in Harrisburg, Pennsylvania, 1944. Received B.A. 1966 and M.A. 1968 from San Diego State University, California. Was resident artist 1971–73 at Patmos Workshop and Gallery, Toronto, Ontario, Canada. Has participated in numerous exhibitions at, among others, Hunter Museum of Art, Chattanooga, Tennessee; and Dairy Association of the Dominican Republic. Won Merit Award and Purchase Award, Hunter Museum of Art, 1980; and Grand Prize, National Holstein Association Exhibition, 1980. Since 1973 has been assistant professor at Covenant College, Lookout Mountain, Tennessee.

There are chickens in my yard; I put up food from a garden and have a wife who enjoys making quilts, but my native Appalachian neighbor reminds me that I do it all like a "Yankee." Perhaps he is right. During the years I have lived in Chattanooga I have grown fond of this region with its traditions, people, fauna, and flora. Appalachia, like the other places I have lived, has its own kind of richness.

The imagery I work with is thoroughly Appalachian, though certain interests that inform my work are not related exclusively to this area. Concerns with time and the effects of its passing, the varied actions of humans with or upon nature, and the formal structures of my work cannot be directly related to my experience of this region.

In recent years I have frequently used the image of the cow in my paintings and prints. Although such imagery is not peculiar to Appalachia, it is derived from it. My interest in the animal began when I was young and employed on a dairy. The sturdy, nonheroic, "feet in the mud" character of Holstein cows with their large size and random markings asks to be painted. I have a respect for the way the Dutch artists Cuyp and Potter rendered the cow as always at home on the earth.

54.
Holstein Drinking   1979
oil on canvas
72 × 48 (182.9 × 121.9)

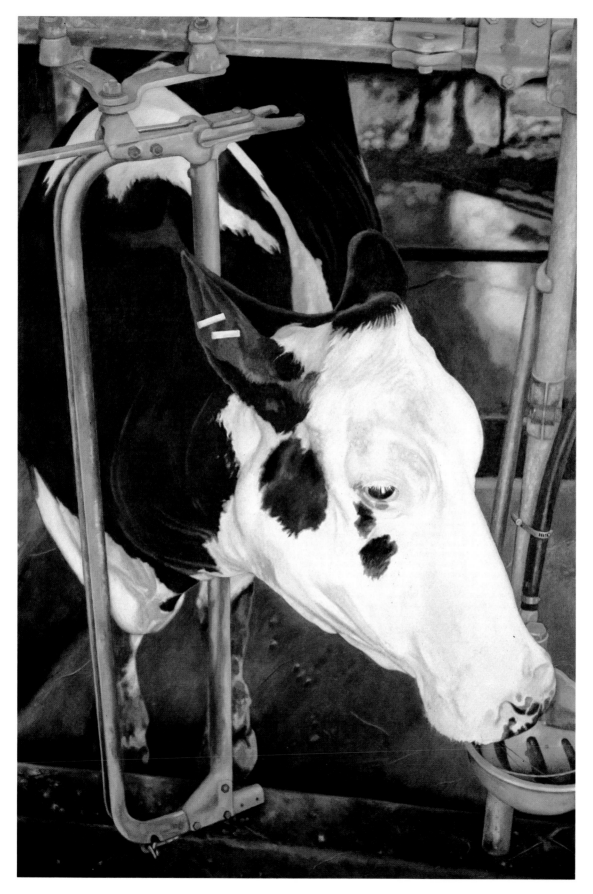

John W. Kortlander

Born in Austin, Texas, 1958. Attended
Ohio University, Athens, 1976–77 and
1978–81. Received cash award, Ohio State
Fair, 1980, and honorable mention, Un-
dergraduate Art League Exhibit, Ohio
University, 1980. Awarded Edna Way
Achievement Scholarship, Ohio Univer-
sity, 1980–81. Lives in Athens, Ohio.

*The Appalachian area in which I have lived most of my life
has had an enormous influence on my work. Its unusual and
irregular configuration of hills and valleys calls one's attention
to the study of spatial organization, while the daily and seasonal changes of color (both sky and earth) make one aware
of the variety and nuances of color that may be found in nature. Moreover, the countryside here, although ruggedly hilly,
does not have the overwhelming scale of the mountains of the
West; more intimate, it is thus easier to grasp, to enter into,
psychologically as well as physically.*

*Although I am not unfamiliar with the art of the past and the
present, the roots of my painting remain Appalachian—the
part of Appalachia that is isolated and remote; that seems lost
in time; and that lends itself to the contemplation of nature
and thus, perhaps, to a greater understanding of man.*

55.
Appalachian Landscape   1980
figure 20 (color)
acrylic on canvas
48 × 54 (121.9 × 137.2)

William Kortlander

Born in Grand Rapids, Michigan, 1925.
Received B.A. 1949 from Michigan State
University, East Lansing, and M.A. 1954
and Ph.D 1958 in art history, from University of Iowa, Iowa City. Taught at
Lawrence University, Appleton, Wisconsin, 1954–56; University of Texas, Austin,
1956–61; and Michigan State University,
summer 1960. Has had numerous one-man
exhibitions, including one in 1974 at
Springfield Art Center, Ohio, and has participated in group exhibitions, including
one at Roanoke Museum of Fine Arts,
Virginia, 1980. Numerous awards include
Painting of the Year Award, "Art Across
America," Knoedler Gallery, New York
City, 1965; and Baker Award for study
and travel in Europe, 1967. Is widely collected. Since 1969 has been professor of
art, Ohio University, Athens.

Living in the hilly Appalachian area of southern Ohio has obviously influenced my choice of subject matter. Anyone who enjoys nature must be captivated by the beauties of this region. When I moved here twenty years ago, I found the greens of summer at first too green; then I began to respond to them and to the rich darks of the shade. Autumn is brilliant and even winter, often mild, has a remarkable range of color (its ochres, siennas, purples, grays, and blacks interrupted by occasional snows). Spring is lovely everywhere, of course, but here it is incomparable, from the first ruddy glow of budding trees to the delicate veils of golden green and on through the whites, pinks, and magentas of blossoming fruit trees, dogwood, redbud, and wild flowers.

From my house on a hilltop, I am constantly aware of the sky, its changes and moods. Days that would be dreary in town are beautiful here, for light modified by atmosphere and the time of day alters the colors and shapes—the entire character—of these ridges and hollows dramatically. Pale grasses take on a metallic sheen against a gray sky, dull tree trunks turn black or violet in the rain.

This landscape is intimate, thus comprehensible; it does not overwhelm despite the arresting configurations of the hills. It lends itself to contemplation and interpretation. The silence and the isolation play a part, too. My work does relate quite directly to the conditions of my life; if I had not moved to this house in the country where I now live, I would have been concerned with other matters in my painting, as I have been in the past.

56.
Distant Horse 1980
acrylic on canvas
48 × 54 (121.9 × 137.2)
Lent by Haber/Theodore Gallery, New York, New York

Ron Kroutel

Born in Chicago, Illinois, 1935. Received B.F.A. 1958 from School of the Art Institute of Chicago (through University of Chicago); and M.F.A. 1963 from University of Michigan, Ann Arbor. Taught in Detroit, Michigan, at Marygrove College, 1963–66; and Society of Arts and Crafts, 1963–66. Has exhibited in numerous group exhibitions, including "Appalachian Corridors Exhibition 4," Charleston, West Virginia, 1974; "Contemporary Figurative Painting in the Midwest," Madison Art Center, Inc., Wisconsin, 1977; and "Surrealism Now," Spaces Gallery, Cleveland, Ohio, 1979. Has had one-man exhibitions at, among others, Fine Arts Gallery, Ohio State University, Columbus, 1976, and Inaugural Exhibition, Park Forest Art Center, Illinois, 1977. Has won numerous purchase prizes and achievement awards. Since 1966 has taught at Ohio University, Athens, and is currently professor of art there.

57.
Animus I: Athleticism   1974
*figure 15
oil on canvas
39 × 49 (99.1 × 124.5)

58.
Processions   1974
oil on canvas
67 × 72 (170.2 × 182.9)
Lent by Daniel D. Maye and Phillip S. Cooke, Louisville, Kentucky

The landscape my figures move through is the terrain of southeastern Ohio. These hills have permeated my imagination and have become a stage upon which my figures act out their narrative roles. While the incongruous juxtaposition of the beautiful Appalachian hills with the harsh economic realities of the area is clearly apparent to me, it is the terrain that has had a lasting effect on my work. With a sense of place these valleys sustain me and help me objectify my responses to living here.

David "Blue" Lamm

Born in Omaha, Nebraska, 1948. Self-taught. Painted mural for Smithsonian Institution Folklife Festival, 1978. Has participated in group exhibitions and has had one-man exhibitions, including one at 63 Bluxome Gallery, San Francisco, California. Cofounder with Andrew Mitchell Willis of Miners Art Group. Work is in many private collections throughout nation.

60.
Roof Collapse   1978
*figure 8
acrylic on canvasboard
24 × 20 (61x51)
Lent by Phyllis Kern, San Francisco, California

59.
Shuttle Car   1977
acrylic on paper
14 × 20 (35.6 × 50.8)

I am a coal miner and an artist. My art reflects my work and the people I work with. I am active in the union, the UMWA. Many of my paintings are of my fellow workers at the mine or on the picket line. My paintings reflect the struggle of miners through the union for a better life for their families and for safety in the mines. I try to talk to people through my painting, to say something about the life and struggles of coal miners. My paintings are done from the point of view of the miners and not the companies. There is very little art in the coal camps of West Virginia, and even less art that speaks to miners about their lives. I hope my paintings do this.

James K. Loveless

Born in Saginaw, Michigan, 1935. Received A.B. 1957 from DePauw University, Greencastle, Indiana, and M.F.A. 1960 from Indiana University, Bloomington. Taught at Hope College, Holland, Michigan, 1960–64; and University of Kentucky, Lexington, 1964–66. Received Ford Foundation grant, Faculty Development in Humanities, 1969; and Yaddo Fellowship, Saratoga Springs, New York, 1980. Has had one-man exhibitions at Root Art Center, Clinton, New York, 1972; E. H. Little Gallery at Memphis State University, Tennessee, 1977; and Everson Museum of Art of Syracuse and Onondaga County, New York, 1977. Since 1966 has taught at Colgate University, Hamilton, New York.

61.
Chenango Sighting   1980
acrylic on paper
image 18 × 24 (45.7 × 61)

I am interested in restoring to my paintings something of an earlier, more visionary art. Landscapes have been the predominant motif in my work since I returned from traveling through Mexico during the spring of 1973. This choice of subject permits me a more workable strategy in expressing that marvelous, yet melancholy, rift between me and the land, whether here in the countryside of upstate New York, in remembered scenes, or in those inscapes summoned through invention.

Until recently it had seemed to me that a return to the landscape form was culturally played out; there were no new adjectives or symbols (images) emerging from inspired insights gained from careful thought and feeling before visually accessible nature. In my paintings I express my renewed interest in this subject matter by depicting scenes, or what I call "sightings," interrupted by incised notations within an unacknowledging landscape. Although the intagliolike elements literally exist in a separate space, they are intended to operate within the represented image by virtue of the composing act or adjustment itself. The effect is not unlike that in Breughel's Fall of Icarus in which neither the plowing farmer nor the sunlit landscape bear witness to the miraculous event, save by virtue of proximity and appearance alone. Unlike Breughel's narrative paintings, wherein the invented landscape often serves as a husk for fable, my sightings are not about man's presence nor his intrusion upon the land. Despite my interest in the visionary aspect of the imagery in my work, I still hold to painting itself as the supreme value.

David A. Lucas

Born in Haymond, Kentucky, 1948. Attended public schools in Haymond and
Neon, Kentucky, and in New Albany, Indiana. Had first one-man exhibition held
at Coffeetrees gallery in Stewart's department store, Louisville, Kentucky. Lives in
Cromona, Kentucky.

62.
Hoeing Potatoes 1979
oil on canvas
24½ × 35 (62.2 × 88.9)

*Living in Appalachia has given my work direction and an
unlimited range of subjects, imagery, and symbols. Life has
been hard here, but very beneficial; it has brought discipline
to my work. Appalachia is where I was born. No place else
have I felt as close to the people and their way of life, as
close to my environment. The people here are always involved
with the earth in some way or other—mining its surface or
digging underground, farming, hunting, fishing, building
roads, burying the dead, setting fenceposts, etc. Yet I had to
live away from this region for a while. I have strong impressions and images of other places, also, of places in which Appalachia has no part. Some of my works reflect this and
stand apart from my Appalachian heritage.*

Stephen Q. Luckett

Born in Mount Vernon, New York, 1938. Studied painting privately; successfully completed correspondence course in fine arts, 1967. Has exhibited locally, including exhibition at Washington County Museum of Fine Arts, Hagerstown, Maryland, 1968. Lives in Halltown, West Virginia. Is employed as a sign painter and also operates both a grocery store and a tax and bookkeeping service.

63.
The Winner 1975
oil on plywood
24 × 30½ (61 × 77.5)

I moved to West Virginia from New York in 1948. I was ten years old and used to lights day and night. When I arrived on the train at night, I saw nothing but darkness. This was my first introduction to West Virginia. Since then I've become acclimated to the beauties of West Virginia, wild, wonderful West Virginia! My favorite colors are brown-yellow-gold and greens. I think this explains why I love West Virginia and how it has influenced me.

I am a sign painter by profession, but my first love is painting. Whenever I complete a painting, I get a personal satisfaction that has to be experienced to be understood!

Richard Lutzke

Born in Beaver Dam, Wisconsin, 1951.
Received B.F.A. 1973 and M.F.A. 1976
from University of Wisconsin, Milwaukee.
Has exhibited in many group and one-man
exhibitions since 1972. Taught 1976 at
John Michael Kohler Art Center, Sheboy-
gan, Wisconsin, and later worked as
freelance artist and designer. Taught from
fall 1980–spring 1981 at Hagerstown Junior College, Maryland. Currently works as
a graphic designer in South Mountain,
Pennsylvania. Lives in Hagerstown.

64.
Phone Book Collage (Bird's Nest) 1980
construction: varnish, glue, and paper
2 × 4¼ × 4¼ (5.1 × 10.8 × 10.8)

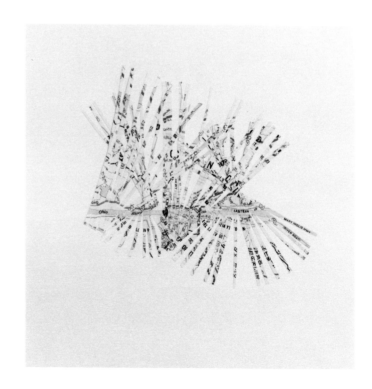

65.
Channeled River 1980
collage: paper on ragboard
4½ × 5 (11.4 × 12.7)

93

Richard Lutzke

Much of the art I make is made from the materials I experience in the routine of everyday life. I prefer such materials to those found only in stores that sell "art supplies" because the former are more universally experienced and recognizable. The materials that I use—pages from telephone books, foliage, newspapers, maps—are often indigenous to this area, but I seldom select them simply because they are unique to a specific locale.

My wife and I moved to western Maryland from the Midwest several years ago. We chose it because it was affordable and close to major centers, and because we had acquaintances here. The geography and culture of this portion of Appalachia did not initially attract us, but they have been significant reasons for our staying.

The specific effect that this particular geography and culture have had upon me is difficult to articulate. Certainly the mountains I see from my window, the pace of life, the friends I have made, and the experiences I have daily, are unique to living here. I am sure they do manifest themselves in my character and work, but to give specific examples would be contrived. They have become part of who I am and the art I make.

66.
Sheet Music 1981
collage: paper on ragboard
12¼ × 9 (31.1 × 22.9)

Ted Metz

Born in Columbus, Ohio, 1949. Received B.A. 1971 from Old Dominion University, Norfolk, Virginia, and M.F.A. 1973 from University of South Carolina, Columbia. Was instructor in technical welding procedures, Rainbow Summer Program, Old Dominion University, 1971. Taught ceramics, Richland County Recreation Commission, Columbia, South Carolina, summer 1973. Served as gallery director, The Gallery, University of Montevallo, Alabama, 1976–78. Was visiting artist, University of Alabama, Tuscaloosa, 1977. Has participated in numerous group exhibitions, including, in Alabama, "The Alabama Sculpture Invitational," Whiting Art Center, Fairhope, 1980; and "The Birmingham Sculpture Invitation," Birmingham Museum of Art, 1978. Has had one-man exhibitions at Mississippi Museum of Art, Jackson, 1978; and Hinds Gallery, Western Carolina University, Cullowhee, North Carolina, 1980. Has received numerous awards and purchase prizes and is widely collected. Since 1973 has been associate professor of art, University of Montevallo, Alabama.

67.
Landscape Progression 1978
stoneware
$18 \times 50\frac{3}{4} \times 36$ ($45.7 \times 128.9 \times 91.4$)
Lent by Birmingham Art Association, Alabama

This piece is a direct sculptural response to a specific landscape. It was inspired by an enormous road cut through Red Mountain in Birmingham, Alabama. I was drawn to the relationship between the subject matter and the materials, and produced sculptures whose subjects were earth forms or earth processes but which were expressed in clay, the earth itself.

I am certain that everything one experiences, including geographic location, will have at least subtle effects upon the creative process. I have lived in Virginia, South Carolina, and Alabama for the majority of my life and all of my creative life. That my work includes—though not exclusively— considerations of the landscape may suggest influences partially based on geography.

The persistent element in my work over the past ten years has been a craftsmanly use of geometric systems as an approach to subject matter. I sometimes take advantage of repetition to develop a progression or transformation. My work evolved from formal nonobjective sculpture in stainless steel and plastics to more literal pieces dealing with the geological landscape and earth processes. These works were largely realized in clay.

Paul Munson

Born in Kokomo, Indiana, 1940. In 1966 received Certificate of Graduation from Detroit Society of Arts and Crafts, Michigan; B.F.A. 1969 from Cranbrook Academy of Art, Bloomfield Hills, Michigan; and M.F.A. 1972 from Virginia Commonwealth University, Richmond. Lectured at Southeastern College Art Conference, Virginia Polytechnic Institute and State University, Blacksburg, Virginia, 1977; and at Sculpture Seminar Invitational, The Southeastern Center for Contemporary Art, Winston-Salem, North Carolina, 1978. Was awarded National Endowment for the Arts Artist's Fellowship, 1979. Has exhibited widely and has received numerous awards, including Certificate of Distinction, Roanoke Museum of Fine Arts, Virginia, 1976. Since 1973 has taught at Radford College, Virginia.

68.
Hatch-Mark 1979
black walnut and organic material
$101 \times 103 \times 46$ ($256.5 \times 261.6 \times 116.8$)

I have lived in Virginia for ten years. I enjoy the Piedmont, mountains, atmosphere, people, and history. I have found the mountains a source for many of my personal ideas and reflections. The Appalachian region has had a strong influence and impact on my life and work.

Nall

Born in Troy, Alabama, 1948. Received
B.A. 1970 from University of Alabama,
Tuscaloosa, and studied 1971–74 at Ecole
des Beaux Arts, Paris, France. Has had
numerous exhibitions at, among others,
Galerie Artpresse International, Nice,
France, 1976; Heirloom Gallery, Arab, Al-
abama, 1977; Huntsville Museum of Art,
Alabama, 1978 and 1981; Galeria II
Traghetto, Venice, Italy, 1979; Galerie Bi-
jan Aalam, Paris, France, 1980; and Grand
Prix "Signature" for Drawing, Nice,
Brignolle, Paris, 1980. Divides time be-
tween Arab, Alabama, and Paris, France.

69.
Alice I   1977
from "Metamorphosis Series"
etching on paper
sheet 24 × 30¼ (61 × 76.8)
Lent from Collection of Huntsville Museum of Art, Alabama

70.
Alice II   1977
see also figure 13
from "Metamorphosis Series"
etching on paper
two sheets: each sheet 24 × 30¼
(61 × 76.8)
Lent from Collection of Huntsville Museum of Art, Alabama

lefthand print

71.
Alice III   1977
from "Metamorphosis Series"
etching on paper
sheet 30¼ × 24 (76.8 × 61)
Lent from Collection of Huntsville Museum of Art, Alabama

72.
Alice IV   1977
from "Metamorphosis Series"
etching on paper
sheet 24 × 30¼ (61 × 76.8)
Lent from Collection of Huntsville Museum of Art, Alabama
(above)

73.
Alice V   1977
from "Metamorphosis Series"
etching on paper
sheet 24 × 30¼ (61 × 76.8)
Lent from Collection of Huntsville Museum of Art, Alabama

Andy Nasisse

Born in Pueblo, Colorado, 1946. Received B.F.A. 1969 from Adams State College, Alamosa, Colorado; and M.F.A. 1973 from University of Colorado, Boulder. Also studied at Instituto Allende, San Miguel De Allende, Mexico; and The Art Institute of Chicago, Illinois. Received Ford Foundation research grant, 1978–81, and National Endowment for the Arts Regional Fellowship, 1979. Has participated in numerous one-man and group exhibitions. In 1980 was selected from national competition for an architectural commission at Atlanta Hartsfield International Airport. Was director of ceramics, Evanston Art Center, Illinois, 1973–76. Taught at University of Colorado, 1972–73, and University of Chicago, Illinois, 1975. Since 1976 has taught at University of Georgia, Athens, and is currently assistant professor of art there. During 1979–80 also served on faculty of University of Georgia Studies Abroad, Cortona, Italy.

74.
Harriet's Power   1980
ceramic and enamel
$14 \times 120 \times 120$ ($35.6 \times 304.8 \times 304.8$)

Harriet's Power is a tribute to Harriet Powers, a slave who lived here in Athens (Georgia), and in the late 1800s produced several beautiful narrative appliqué quilts. The piece is one of a series of large works that are partially inspired by examples of very old quilts in which areas of geometric patterns have begun to decay, exposing the organic-looking matrix or batting beneath. I try to set up a system by which several layers of pattern can exist in a stratification, relating to each other in a casual and sometimes unexpected way.

After the Civil War, the southern Appalachians were, for the most part, by-passed by America's industrial expansion. This isolation contributed to a stronger sense of continuity in the folk customs of this area and to abundant evidence of a very rich material culture.

The people of southern Appalachia are close to the land. Their religious beliefs are often a function more of direct experience than faith, and there seems to be more evidence of, and tolerance for, individual idiosyncrasy. Consequently, there ex-ist numerous examples of folk and naïve art ranging from incredible fantasy environments to imaginative whirligigs and on to some very beautiful and subtle examples of Early American quilts. I've been deeply affected by the directness and honesty of the work of untrained artists, and am especially impressed with what seems to be an obsessive or compulsive need to embellish and decorate. Pattern takes on meaning of itself, and decoration can become a vehicle for transcendence in some work by visionaries and primitives.

Jerry L. Noe

Born in Harlan County, Kentucky, 1940. Received B.A. 1963 from University of Kentucky, Lexington, and M.F.A. 1970 from School of the Art Institute of Chicago, Illinois. Taught 1963–66 in Harlan County (Kentucky) School System. Since 1967 has exhibited in group exhibitions throughout United States. Has had one-man exhibitions at 55 Mercer Gallery, New York City; Henri Gallery, Washington, D.C.; University of Kentucky; and North Carolina Museum of Art, Raleigh. Has received many awards and fellowships, including National Endowment for the Arts Southeastern Artist Fellowship, 1976. Since 1972 has taught at University of North Carolina, Chapel Hill. Lives in Cawood, Kentucky, and in Chapel Hill.

75.
Mountain Landscape with Rainbow   1980
figure 2
wood, neon, and paint
36 × 48 × 4⅜ (91.4 × 121.9 × 11.1)

Growing up in Appalachia has probably been influential to me in my work in at least two ways. First, there is the physical environment of the mountains. I grew up on a hill looking out at mountains in literally every direction—north, east, south, west. I saw the sun rise over the mountains, the sun set over the mountains, the rain and rainbows over the mountains. The natural undulating arches and curves of the mountain landscape have repeatedly cropped up in my work, often in an unconscious way, regardless of what media I worked in and what my conscious goals were at the time. Second, there is the ingenuity fostered by the Appalachian way of life. I grew up in a fairly isolated environment, making my own toys without kits or instruction booklets (I was always a maker). I also grew up without any ideas about what art was supposed to be (I never saw an original work of art, and few reproductions, until I was seventeen or eighteen). When I began to study art formally, then, I was not encumbered by traditional concepts and could approach my work with freshness of vision.

David Parrish

Born in Birmingham, Alabama, 1939. Received B.F.A. 1961 from University of Alabama, Tuscaloosa. Has had one-man exhibitions at, among others, Galerie François Petit, Paris, France, 1973; Huntsville Museum of Art, Alabama; and Nancy Hoffman Gallery, New York City, 1981. Group exhibitions include "Super Realism," The Baltimore Museum of Art, Maryland, 1975; "Painting and Sculpture Today," Indianapolis Museum of Art, Indiana, 1981; "Aspects of Photorealism," Randolph-Macon Women's College, Lynchburg, Virginia, 1980; and "Contemporary American Realism Since 1960," Pennsylvania Academy of The Fine Arts, Philadelphia, 1981–83 (to travel in U.S. and Europe). Lives in Huntsville, Alabama.

76.
KAYO 1976
oil on canvas
51¼ × 76 (130.2 × 193)
Lent by Nancy Hoffman Gallery, New York, New York

Gary E. Pettigrew

Born in Boulder, Colorado, 1935. Received B.F.A. 1958 from University of Colorado, Boulder, and M.F.A. 1963 from Ohio University, Athens. Has exhibited at Capricorn Galleries, Bethesda, Maryland; Weintraub Galleries, New York City; The Butler Institute of American Art, Youngstown, Ohio; and many others. Awards include Strathmore Award, The Butler Institute of American Art; Baker Fund Award, Ohio University; and B. F. Goodrich Purchase Award, Akron Art Museum, Ohio. Since 1962 has taught at Ohio University.

77.
Custodian   1979
acrylic on ragboard
19 × 25 (48.3 × 63.5)
Lent by Capricorn Galleries, Bethesda, Maryland

Lester F. Pross

Born in Bristol, Connecticut, 1924. Received B.A. 1945 and M.A. 1946 from Oberlin College, Ohio. Since 1946 has taught in Art Department, Berea College, Kentucky. Received Haskell Traveling Fellowship, Oberlin College, 1957–58; and Fulbright teaching fellowship, University of the Punjab, Lahore, Pakistan, 1957–58. Exhibitions include "Midstates Annual," Evansville, Indiana, 1964; "Face of Kentucky I and II Traveling Exhibition," 1968–70; "Appalachian Corridors Exhibition 2" (opened Charleston, West Virginia, traveled), 1970; and "Kentucky Bicentennial," 1974. Was visiting professor of art, American University, Cairo, Egypt, 1967–68. Is currently professor of art at Berea College and since 1950 has been chairman of its Art Department.

Appalachia's rhythms are the subjects and themes of my paintings; I find them not only in my Kentucky pictures but also in those I painted about New York, Maine, and Japan. The rhythms are, of course, universal. Seeing them so clearly in Twin, Indian Fort, and Bear mountains, and in the fields in my own backyard, allows me to see them also in Bleeker and Speculator and Bigelow mountains, and in Momoyama and Hieizan and Silk Hat Mountain. Kentucky's horizons go with me. I see them from a distance, with a horizon view, rather than intimately and from the valleys. I like the larger view, the sense of the variety and order of forms and rhythms, the boldness and subtleties and colors, the large shapes and flattened spaces. I enjoy the changes brought by the weather, the hours, and the seasons. I live in these mountains, and they are my paintings.

78.
Woodlot 1973
figure 3
oil on canvas
16 × 30 (40.6 × 76.2)

Robert T. Reedy

Born in Richmond, California, 1952. Received B.F.A. 1974 and M.F.A. 1977 from University of Mississippi, University. Studied ceramics at Penland School of Crafts, North Carolina, summers 1978 and 1979. Has given many workshops and short-term courses. Has been included in numerous group exhibitions and has received many awards. Has had one-man exhibitions at, among others, University of Mississippi, 1974, and Delaware State Arts Council, Lewes, 1976. Since 1978 has been instructor in ceramics and sculpture at Itawamba Junior College, Fulton, Mississippi. Lives in Mantachie, Mississippi.

Living in Mississippi has definitely influenced me and my work! For years as a student I struggled to find a direction or source for my ceramics. I realize now that I was trying too hard to "make" art. Everyone seemed to be looking to New York for inspiration and images, but I didn't feel comfortable with these. Growing up and living in Mississippi have nothing to do with New York. Granted there are similarities, but where can you eat catfish and hushpuppies in New York? I slowly began to realize that my images should be coming from the environment with which I was most familiar— Mississippi.

In my work the stories and the placement of my forms and images are just as important as the aesthetic concepts that I use. I hope it is my understanding of my own environment, coupled with a fundamental knowledge of aesthetic values, that will make my work unique to others. No one else touches clay as I do, no one else sees as I do.

My forms are made of clay, slip-decorated and smoke-fired by the raku process. The pieces are taken from the kiln red hot and are reduced in combustible sawdust. My love for raku is strictly because of the process. Although raku is traditionally connected with Zen Buddhism, Zen concepts have nothing to do with my work or lifestyle. As a Mississippian I would find it extremely difficult to imitate Eastern culture or to adopt Eastern values.

79.
Pillows and Divining Rod 1980
smoke-fired raku, slip decorated
each piece 28 × 10 × 7½ (71.1 × 25.4 × 19)
(above, left)

80.
Pillows and Ladder 1980
smoke-fired raku, slip decorated
28 × 10 × 7½ (71.1 × 25.4 × 19)
(above, right)

David L. Riffle

Born in Gassaway, West Virginia, 1947. Studied 1966–67 at West Virginia Institute of Technology, Montgomery, and 1969 at East Carolina University, Greenville, North Carolina. Received B.A. 1975 from West Virginia State College Institute. Has been included in many regional shows. Received Merit Award in "West Virginia Juried Exhibition '79," Charleston, West Virginia, 1979. Has given numerous workshops in West Virginia public schools for both children and adults. Lives in Poca, West Virginia.

Living in Appalachia has meant a lot to me and my art, maybe only because I can live here and paint with the freedom I need. I have a situation in this area that would be very difficult to obtain anywhere else. I can live here and paint while working at part-time jobs to survive.

I was born and raised in West Virginia. I have traveled in several countries and I was also in the Marines and am a Vietnam veteran. Always, however, I got homesick for the beautiful mountains of West Virginia.

I guess the influence of Appalachia is just being happy where I'm at and doing what I enjoy most, painting.

81.
House in Nitro, West Virginia   1979
modeling paste and acrylic on balsa wood
25 × 32 (63.5 × 81.3)

Michael Rogers

Born in Memphis, Tennessee, 1954. Received B.A. 1977 from Le Moyne-Owen College, Memphis, Tennessee. Worked as private art instructor in Memphis, 1979. Has been included in numerous major group exhibitions throughout nation. Has had one-man exhibitions at Le Moyne-Owen College, 1977; Northeast Junior College, Boonesville, Mississippi, 1980; and the Center for the Study of Southern Culture, University of Mississippi, 1981. Works are included in collections of University Museum, University of Mississippi; Mississippi Museum of Art, Jackson; and Le Moyne-Owen College. Since 1978 has been an M.F.A. candidate at University of Mississippi.

82.
The Prodigal Son   1981
oil on canvas
50 × 60 (127 × 152.4)

Certainly one's environment plays an important part in establishing one's thinking and living patterns. With my life thus far having been spent either in Tennessee or in Mississippi (two of the thirteen states of Appalachia), I feel that my art has been influenced to some degree by the characteristic realism of these areas. Their art (not unlike that in much of the South) seems known for its straightforward renderings of rural scenery and for portraits of poor, overworked, elderly members of the local society. Constant exposure to such representational artwork while I was growing up has, no doubt, strongly contributed to my choosing to work in a realistic fashion. My interest in painting people also stems from such exposure. But, whatever links exist, my art could hardly be categorized as "Southern."

My attitude about subject matter or imagery seems also to be derived from exposure to the so-called new realism (often termed super realism, sharp-focus realism, hyper-realism, radical realism, or photographic realism). This contemporary approach to realism generally emphasizes largeness of scale, sharply focused common scenery, and the use of photography.

My personal experiences and surroundings usually provide the foundation for my work. Mere sentimentality, however, is consciously avoided. Oftentimes I strive for photographic effects, while at other times I strive for more naturalistic depictions. My works are usually large-scale oil paintings. The largeness of scale amplifies the structural elements or abstract qualities (shape, line, and color), while the relatively new approach to realism, hyper-realism, adds new significance to the otherwise ordinary depictions.

Edward Rogge

Born in Peoria, Illinois, 1941. Received B.A. in history 1964 from Carthage College, Kenosha, Wisconsin. Spent six years in army, taught in public schools in Springfield, Illinois, took up farming. Currently manages cotton and soybean farm in Kilmichael, Mississippi.

I always wanted to paint but never received the encouragement to do so when I was younger. Now I paint scenes from memories that come flooding back to me when I reflect on my life and the time I have spent among the hills and rivers of the mountain regions of the South, and on the experiences that give so much richness and diversity to life there. My memories are of kind, supportive friends and lazy days spent walking country roads or riding a mule past rail fences as I came to know the land and the people.

83.
Revival 1979
mixed media on watercolor paper
14 × 17½ (35.6 × 44.5)

This scene is of a revival being held at the Mt. Hebron Church of God. Generally speaking, the congregation is composed of Holy Rollers and True Lighters, with a few strays and a Nazarene or two thrown in for good measure. Grover Shayse, Claire and Holly Goodin, Nightmare Alice Rainey, Tinker and Tied-Eye Bright, as well as Pancake and Buttermilk, are in attendance to receive the word of salvation as the Reverend admonishes the last souls to repent. The flock is also being tended by Florence Hosapple, a faith healer adept at the laying on of hands.

The Reverend oftentimes professed to having saved a lot of sinners. He supposedly saved a whole roomful stranded in the upper story of a house in Maysfield, Kentucky, during a time of high water one early spring. Prior to his conversion, the Reverend peddled pearl necklaces door to door. He remarked once that he had crossed the United States twenty-seven times in a Model-T Ford. During his illustrious career he is said to have once ridden out of town beneath a boxcar, the wolves yapping at his heels, when the townspeople discovered that his pearls were made of glass. He is also known to have once been apprehended by a local constable for pushing bogus railroad stock for a nonexistent railroad. Then there is the fight he had awhile back with Jack Dempsey in Salt Lake City over a gypsy dancing girl.

Martin Mosteller got saved once a year and drunk once a year. He said that each experience did him "a hell of a lot of good."

Luther Hicks was at a revival one time held in either Fountain Green or Dallas City, Tennessee. The preacher asked everyone who wanted to go to heaven to stand up. Luther remained seated. When asked if he was a backslider or what and why didn't he stand up and didn't he want to go to heaven, Luther replied that where *he* wanted to go was back home.

Edward Rogge

84.

Trailer Park 1979
mixed media on watercolor paper
15½ × 19½ (39.4 × 49.5)

The inhabitants are occupied with life in this, their own particular domain.

The cosmetics saleslady, Mrs. Prescott, is talking to Rhodella Brown, who may be in the market for some face powder or a bar of scented soap.

René Justice is visiting with Betty La Rue (who once had her picture taken with Tom Mix). Mrs. La Rue is minding her grandson, Booger, who is close behind her pongee housecoat. Carl La Rue, Betty's husband, is tinkering away beneath their Pontiac Chieftain. Carl is a deep-fry cook at the country club.

John Ross stands before the temporarily incapacitated automobile, cleaning his fingernails with a pocketknife before leaving for a rum game in town in the back of Sam Clark's poolroom.

Darrell Swartzer sits reflectively in the doorway of his sister's "home on wheels." Recently arrived from Texas, he has been busily sizing up job prospects—and Lila Backs, the black sheep of a well-to-do "Dutch" (German) farmer. He and Lila ran into one another at the Villa tavern in town.

W. A. Maurer, who owns the forge and tinshop across the river, is locally respected as an astute businessman.

Art Rosenbaum

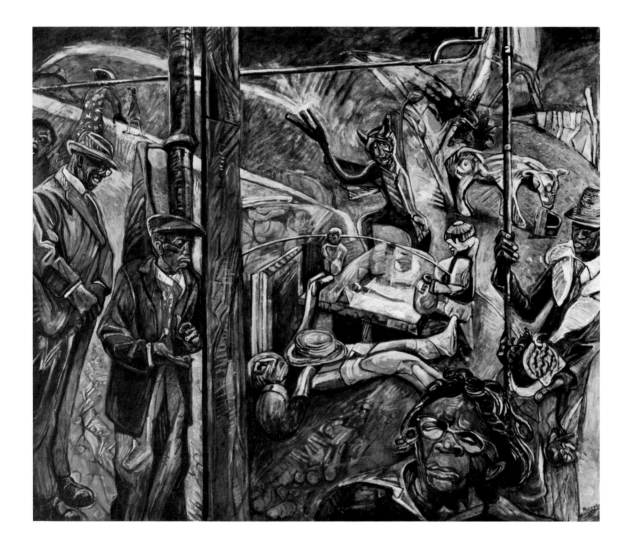

85.
Mr. Hall's Devil and Drunkards in Concrete, with Deacon Gates, Deacon Ferrell, and the Gilmores   1979
oil and alkyd resin on canvas
60 × 72 (152.4 × 182.9)

Born in Ogdensburg, New York, 1938. Received B.A. 1960 and M.F.A. 1961 from Columbia University, New York City. Awarded Boar's Head Poetry Prize, Columbia University, 1957; and Fulbright painting fellowship, Institut d'Art et d'Archeologie, Paris, France, 1964–65. Received grant from National Endowment for the Arts (NEA) to record and paint northern Georgia folklore. Participated 1978 in "Folk Visions and Voices," an exhibition partially supported by NEA, based on northern Georgia folklore and accompanied by live performances of Ameri-

can traditional music, Athens, Georgia. Also exhibited in Cortona, Italy, 1978; New York City, 1979; and Atlanta, Georgia, 1980. Since 1961 has made ten albums of field recordings of American traditional music and three albums of original music: *Five-String Banjo and Art of the Mountain Banjo*, 1972; *Art Rosenbaum and Al Murphy*, 1976; and *Georgia Banjo Blues*, 1981. Since 1976 has been assistant professor of art, Department of Art, University of Georgia, Athens.

Art Rosenbaum

86.
Harvey and George Childers, Pickens County, Georgia 1980
charcoal on paper
22 × 26 (55.9 × 66)

During the years when I was growing up in Indianapolis, my interest in mountain banjo tunes and songs brought me into contact with migrant musicians from east Kentucky and Tennessee. From these people, Edward Ward, Shorty and Juanita Sheehan, Dallas Henderson, to name a few, I learned much, part of which was that I could find in the power, the lyricism, and the humor of their music a correlative and an inspiration for the visual imagery I was developing in my painting.

My art and my interest in traditional mountain music and culture have developed in parallel fashion since that time, and since moving to north Georgia, I have formed close artistic and musical associations with many mountain families and individuals who continue to carry on and develop the special culture of the region. Again I should name some names: The Ellers of Towns Country, in whose music and way of life both the generosity and the fierce independence of mountain culture is exemplified; Jake Staggers, a black banjo picker of Toccoa who played for hundreds of black dances in the Piedmont and white dances up in the mountains, and who can still coax some rare preblues tunes from his arthritic fingers; Maud "Granny" Thacker of Tate, winemaker, buck dancer, and singer with the finest repertoire of old British and early American ballads I have met with in the Georgia Blue Ridge; the Reverend Howard Finster, visionary folk painter and environmental artist, singer, and banjo picker, a man whose varied artistic productions synthesize elements of folk verbal and oral culture with his unique imagination and vis-

ual sense; W. Guy Bruce, musician, watch repairman, storyteller of Trion, who brought his eighty-five years' worth of wit and music to the Smithsonian Folklife Festival last year; Ross Brown, fiddler of Hiawassee, who when he says "I don't care nothin' about up-to-date" means not that he wants to return to the past but that he is refusing to accept a Nashville-or Hollywood-imposed definition of his music and culture.

I find in Appalachian culture not a sentimental nostalgic escape into an earlier way of life, but a culture developed in adversity that continues to change and still has much to say to Americans in the last decades of the twentieth century. Living and working among the bearers of mountain culture has certainly given energy to my own art. I appreciate what Bob Norman wrote about my work in a New York show a few years ago: "Art Rosenbaum finds beauty, weirdness, and sensuality in folklore and is not afraid to show it to us in our . . . jet-age world." My friend Andy Nasisse has some dazzling folk quilts on his wall and uses them as a kind of gage of his own art, saying that he will reject anything of his own that is less interesting than the quilts. I feel similarly: my paintings must honestly reflect the faces and environments of the mountain musicians who are my friends and subjects. They must also express through color and painted gesture and pattern the energy and complexity that can be found in a Gordon Tanner fiddle performance or a camp-meeting song sung by Laethe Eller. If they don't, it's time to start over.

110

Carolyn C. Sanders-Turner

88.
River Road 1979
watercolor on paper
21⅜ × 29 (54.3 × 73.7)

Born in Evanston, Illinois, 1947. Received A.F.A. 1967 from Sullins College, Bristol, Virginia, and studied 1977–79 at Concord College, Athens, West Virginia. Taught drawing, Antioch College, Beckley Branch, Beckley, West Virginia, 1976. Has exhibited widely in Southeast, in, among others, "Southern Watercolor Society Annual Exhibitions," 1980 and 1981; "Baltimore Watercolor Society Regional Exhibitions," 1979 and 1980; and "Aqueous '80," Louisville, Kentucky. Has received numerous awards and purchase prizes, including first in painting, "Chemical City Festival," West Virginia, 1979 and 1980.

87.
Forgotten Treasures 1980
★figure 9 (color)
watercolor on paper
21½ × 29 (54.6 × 73.7)

Duuring the seven years I have spent in West Virginia I've come to appreciate many traditional art forms, especially handcrafts. As a result I have begun incorporating many of them, mainly crocheting and quilting, both symbolically and realistically into my paintings.

Most of my paintings have dealt with women; their varied and hidden existences, fantasies, and trappings. Through my relationships with some of the women living in the mountains in extremely limiting conditions, I've come to recognize how isolated from outside stimulus it is possible to be in today's world. Yet there is a continuity between generations, support systems within their families that many of us have never known. Also, there is so much creativity in everyday activities—activities that wouldn't generally be identified as "fine art."

At this time the two interests—women and their more traditional handwork—are intertwining in my work, as exemplified in my "Lace Curtain" series. I find the slower pace and comparative isolation of the region are conducive to my spending the large amounts of time I need to devote to painting; they also help promote independent expression and progression in my art.

111

Mary Shelley

Born in Doylestown, Pennsylvania, 1950. Received B.A. 1972 from Cornell University, Ithaca, New York. Has exhibited in numerous exhibitions since 1974. Work is included in The American Museum in Britain, Bath, England. Was artist in residence at Artpark, Lewistown, New York, 1977; at Taughannock Falls State Park, Trumansburg, New York, 1977; and at Chenango Falls State Park, Chenango Falls, New York, 1979. Received grants from National Landmark Society of Ithaca, New York, 1979; and America the Beautiful Fund, 1980. Currently works as sign carver. Lives in West Danby, New York.

90.
Busy Bee Diner   1980
*figure 6
carved, painted wood
25 × 24 (63.5 × 61)
Lent by Stephen Mader, Syracuse, New York

I never used to think that I could draw. I never had art training. I started doing my carvings when my father sent me a carved picture he had made of me, as a little girl at the farm where I grew up. I liked what he had done so much that I decided to do one of my own. At that time I was trying to be a writer, so naturally I took a story out of my life and set it down in picture form. Soon I had so much more reaction to my "picture" stories that I stopped writing and kept carving.

Drawing has always been the hardest part for me. I usually wait until I have a clear picture in my mind of what I want to do. Then I set the drawing down as quickly as I can. Afterwards I transfer it to my wood with carbon paper. My work is entirely carved with no glued-on pieces. I use white pine or basswood, several boards fastened together by battens on the back. I paint the finished carving with acrylics, and afterwards varnish it. I have been working at this art form for eight years and in this time have done about one hundred and twenty painted woodcarvings.

89.
Cows and Milk   1979
carved, painted wood
17½ × 16¾ (44.5 × 42.5)
Lent by Richard and Lois Rosenthal, Cincinnati, Ohio

Elizabeth W. Shumacker

Born in Chattanooga, Tennessee, 1912. Received B.A. 1934 from University of Chattanooga and studied at Hunter Museum of Art, Chattanooga. Has exhibited widely since 1948 and has received numerous awards. Work was chosen by U.S. Department of State for inclusion in Art-in-the-Embassies Program, 1967. Taught 1955–75 at Chattanooga Art Institute of Hunter Museum of Art. Was visiting instructor in Chattanooga at University of Chattanooga, 1969, and at University of Tennessee, 1973 and 1975. Has exhibited at Hunter Museum of Art and in many other locations. Has won numerous awards and prizes and is represented in many public and private collections, including Hunter Museum of Art and The High Museum of Art, Atlanta, Georgia.

91.
Abstract Hereafter   1970
polymer on raw linen
46 × 38 (116.8 × 96.5)

Linda R. Sokolowski

92.
*The Grassed Terrace of an Abandoned
Space* 1978
oil on canvas
28 × 34 (71.1 × 86.4)
Lent by Kraushaar Galleries, New York,
New York

Born in Utica, New York, 1943. Received
B.F.A. 1965 from Rhode Island School of
Design, Providence, and M.A. 1970 (under Mauricio Lasansky) and M.F.A. 1971
from University of Iowa, Iowa City. Received Carnegie Grant, 1965; State University of New York Research Grant, 1976;
and Childe Hassam Purchase Award from
American Academy And Institute of Arts
And Letters, 1978. One-man exhibitions
include "The Bathers," Kraushaar Galleries, New York City, 1976; "Linda So-
kolowski: The Graphic Works,
1972–1977," University Art Gallery, State
University of New York at Binghamton,
1978; and a selection of paintings, drawings, prints, architectural gardens, still
lifes, and portraits, Kraushaar Galleries,
1979. Since 1970 has participated in numerous national and state group exhibitions. Currently is associate professor of
art, State University of New York at
Binghamton.

93.
Segovian Light and Trees 1979
oil wash and pastel on paper
29 × 41 (73.66 × 104.14)
Lent by Kraushaar Galleries, New York,
New York

*Uninhabited landscapes possess an ancient history even if
they are young, a kind of mystical power that holds a difficult
magic over the work. Their ruins are more real, more alive
and contemporary, then twenty-first-century architecture. Their
trees grow, their slopes shape with a formality appropriate to
their nature. They allow a vision of a larger world, one that
isn't yet beside the one that is. The part that "isn't" has to be
as convincing to the maker-viewer as the tangible side. The
former is perhaps the spirit of the work generously given by
that which can constantly be seen reinvented.*

*Here in upstate New York exists the strange sight of crum-
bling health spas used by wealthy tourists in 1920, vacation
spots left to collapse on their own. There are hundreds of un-
used old hotels. Often, in off-season in a summer resort town,
one gets the feeling the people left just yesterday, that impend-
ing disaster forced a hasty exodus. The warning always seems
to have come in time. The interior spaces continue to wait for
the people to return. These places are slightly decadent, contemporary Pompeiis without the beauty or the cultural background. Yet they exist with a weighted presence. There is a
strong element of time held inside their boundaries.*

John Spofforth

Born in Saint Paul, Minnesota, 1931. Received B.F.A. 1962 and M.F.A. 1968 from Ohio University, Athens. Served as sculpture consultant, Central Waterfront Planning Committee, Toronto, Ontario, Canada, 1974. Was curator of Visual Resources, College of Fine Arts, Ohio University, 1968–70. Was visiting artist in sculpture, University of Alabama, Birmingham, 1974–75. Has received numerous grants from National Endowment for the Arts and Ohio Arts Council. Work was included in "Appalachian Corridors Exhibition 1" and "2," 1968 and 1970 (opened Charleston, West Virginia; traveled); the "Blossom-Kent Outdoor Sculpture Invitational," Ohio, 1970, 1972, and 1973; and "In the Summer of 1980: Statewide Sculpture Competition" Ohio State University Gallery of Fine Art, Columbus, 1980. Has received numerous commissions and work is included in many public and private collections. Lives in Athens, Ohio.

The contrast of the treacherous boulder cliffs and craggy hillsides of the meandering countryside to the lush, level farmlands of the Appalachian region has critically influenced my aesthetic preference for tactile organic form, irregular contours, nonhorizontal and nonvertical relationships of line and mass in my work. Rough texture, earth colors, geological stress-line pattern, close-up feeling of presence, a naturalistic sense of placement—these elements are part and parcel of Appalachia and are expressed in one's daily life. They have become formal elements in my brick forms, psychologically and metamorphically suggesting that such features are universally characteristic of lives fully lived and forms not merely of the cerebral studio atmosphere but also of life deeply felt.

I come from the West and Midwest, where the land is flat and evenly laid out, and the sky is a big top half of one's perceptual experience, but Athens, the home of Ohio University, has become after twenty-five years my "soul home." I completed undergraduate and graduate art training at Ohio University and worked eight years at professional bricklaying and house remodeling in the Athens area. After receiving my M.F.A. in 1968, I stayed in Athens to transform my art training and bricklaying into a personalized, fresh approach to environmental sculpture, to ideas of structurally integrated physical form.

The high and low hills and fields of Appalachia, the weathered trees and buildings, the loneness of fog and rain have influenced my "Towers" series of irregularly stacked, highrising, clustered brick and mortar column forms. The prehistoric Indian mounds have greatly influenced my "Ancient Hump Ring" idea. This irregularly coiling, serpentine, ringlike form suggests associations with the ancient idea of the unity of the circle in the midst of raw nature.

As with the Indian feeling for ancient myth, I feel sculpture, especially, must relate physically to people's environments not only as afterthoughts attached to large, anonymous architectural structures, but as structurally, physically integrated components within our midst, in our daily lives. The sense of "personal," of persona, *gained from Appalachia imbues my work with a need to be connected with and become a part of a particular place.*

94.
Untitled
construction: brick and mortar
to be constructed by artist at site of exhibition from prepared plans

Robert Stark

Born in Sidney, New York, 1939. Received B.A. 1964 from University of Denver, Colorado. Studied restoration and conservation of painting 1971–74 with Robert Scott Wiles at Corcoran Gallery of Art, Washington, D.C. Has exhibited in Washington, D.C., galleries since 1967. Has had one-man exhibitions at Corcoran Gallery of Art, 1969, and The Phillips Collection, Washington, D.C., 1979. Is represented in numerous collections, including, in New York City, The Museum of Modern Art, and in Washington, D.C., The Phillips Collection; National Museum of American History, Smithsonian Institution; and collection of *Washington Post*. Lives and works in Union Dale, Pennsylvania.

95.
Millstream X 1979
oil on linen
28 × 36 (71 × 91.5)
Lent by John P. Forest, D.D.S., Annandale, Virginia

My ties to this mountainous corner of rural northeastern Pennsylvania are those of childhood, family, and years of painting and photographing its familiar landscape. I returned here in the midsixties after finishing college to work at my art, left after a few years, and then returned again with my wife to buy an empty general store and convert it into our home and studios.

As a child I knew Union Dale as a busy farming community with three general stores where you could buy everything from your food and clothes to a new tractor. Farmers still brought their milk to the creameries every day, some still using horses. There was a railroad station, hotel, a water-powered feedmill, a lumberyard, a library, and much more.

I returned to find much of this vitality faded, businesses and farms left empty through age and attrition. It was rather a bleak prospect made agreeable only by old family ties and the natural beauty.

But all of that has gradually changed. In the past dozen years, artists, musicians, writers, and craftspeople have begun to find their way here, trading the cultural abundance of the city for the freedom to work without distraction, and in turn

Robert Stark

becoming part of the fabric of the community and its growth.

I believe that the artist is an extension of his (or her) family and community, that his work is a reflection of the tone and nature of its values, both real and abstract, and that his success lies in the ability to bring art and life together, creating new foundations for the future.

96.
The Artist's Garden 1977
oil on jute
36¼ × 52¾ (92 × 134)
Lent by Charles de Limur, San Francisco,
California

F. Clark Stewart

Born in Evansville, Indiana, 1942. Received B.A. 1964 from University of Redlands, California, and M.F.A. 1966 from Claremont Graduate School, California. Has been included in many major exhibitions and collections. Has had one-man exhibitions at several colleges, universities, and museums in South and in 1980 at American Gallery, Bern, Switzerland. Received two University of Tennessee research grants: one in 1967–68 to explore work in acrylic plastic, and one in 1970 to publish a limited edition of interpretive drawings for William Blake's *Marriage of Heaven and Hell*. Since 1966 has taught at University of Tennessee, Knoxville.

97.
Darkpool   1978
*figure 16
wood, paper, and foamcore board
24 × 7½ × 4½ (61 × 19 × 11.4)

98.
Trigolithic Troglodytes   1979
acrylic, Xerox, and foil on paper
15½ × 22⅜ (39.4 × 56.8)

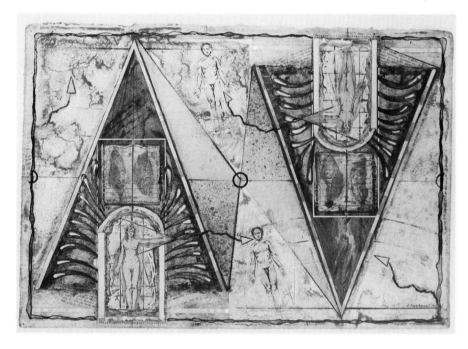

Though Appalachia sometimes manifests itself in negative ways (for example, the redneck image), it also foments a climate in which personal artistic idiosyncrasy is perhaps easier to maintain than in the atmosphere of the compelling artistic currents of more sophisticated areas. In my case I feel this had led to a closer exploration inward rather than development of an outward-oriented viewpoint. Among the personality stereotypes of the region that I value is that imbedded in a sense of hyper-individualism.

A trait of the region that has proved an irritant to me is the greater tolerance there today for the shoddy and temporized solution to craftsmanship in objects drawn from everyday life. My annoyance at this has probably caused me to give greater importance to the craftsmanship of making art than I might have otherwise. I must admit, however, to a certain fascination with the often unanticipated and spontaneous relationships that the "make-do" approach generates.

Any assessment of the effect on my work of my east Tennessee Appalachian environment must note the lush, closed density of the landscape space and atmosphere. Rather than confrontations with panoramic vistas, my eye became drawn to small confined areas rich in variety and detail. In my work the priority has shifted towards a development of complex, focused surfaces. It has been my observation that this tendency is one shared by many regional artists. The confinement of space in the mountain-forest thickets that I find very appealing has probably strengthened my concern for making art in which containment is an important concern.

Joe W. Thrasher

Born in West Blocton, Alabama, 1934. Attended public schools in West Blocton. Participated in Special Studies Program, University of Alabama, University, 1980. Lives in Adamsville, Alabama.

99.
Man and his Soul   1980
carved wood
man: 24½ × 6 × 4 (62.2 × 15.2 × 10.2)
soul: 12¾ × 6 × 4 (32.4 × 15.2 × 10.2)

I *was born into poverty and grew up in a country home in a thinly populated county of Alabama. Life then and there was less complicated but, most important for my work, the approach to life was on a simpler plane.*

In a poor family, in a basically poor county, simplicity and improvisation were a way of life through necessity, not desire. This simple approach, ingrained in my very soul during the first two decades of my life, has made itself felt in my carving and, in this respect, life in Appalachia has most strongly influenced my work.

I believe I follow the pattern unconsciously set by the majority of self-trained Appalachian carvers with this background who have remained true to their heritage. Function—in this case, basic image—has always maintained its prime importance. Detail beyond that required to reinforce and identify the image has remained secondary. Finishes are integrated parts, used to emphasize the natural grain and color of the wood and provide protection, but they do not distract from the work by their own beauty.

My work could well be called "primitive" without insult, for *it represents the uninhibited and spontaneous outlook and self-trained approach of one who still sees life in the simple manner to which he was born. I carve as I see the world and the objects in it.*

This same approach is reflected in all of my works—my painting and my poetry—all of which intermingle at times. The name for the work in this exhibition came, in fact, from one of my original poems:

In a dream I was standing in a meadow
   White clover beneath my feet,
When from somewhere beyond the gates of eternity
   A voice came back from time.
It fell on my ear with the force of a mighty wind—
   Yet with the calmness of a summer breeze
The voice had claimed the judgment
   And how it was going to be
By the purity of a virgin
   And the innocence of a child.
And I cried "Oh, voice—what of me and my soul?"
   And the voice replied—
"Judge yourself guilty—And innocent you shall be."

Stanley D. Townsend

Born in Princeton, Indiana, 1947. Received B.F.A. 1972 from East Tennessee State University, Johnson City. Through grant from Georgia Council for the Arts and National Endowment for the Arts (NEA), served as artist in residence at Creative Arts Guild, Inc., Dalton, Georgia, 1975; and through grant from Tennessee Arts Commission and NEA served as artist in residence at Hunter Museum of Art, Chattanooga, Tennessee, 1977. Has exhibited widely, with works included in "American Bicentennial Revolution Art Exhibition," Nashville, Tennessee, 1976; and "Southeastern Graphics Invitational," The Mint Museum of Art, Charlotte, North Carolina, 1979. Is represented in Tennessee State Museum, Nashville, and American Association of Colleges and Universities, Washington, D.C. Since 1970 has taught at Hunter Museum School of Art.

I *am sure that living in the Appalachia region has had an influence on my work. How? That can only be seen by viewing the work, not by words.*

100.
Eggs   1977
graphite on paper
13 × 22 (33 × 55.9)
Lent by Mrs. Alice Townsend, Signal Mountain, Tennessee

Barry Vance

Born in Baltimore, Maryland, 1946. Received B.F.A. 1969 from Pratt Institute, Brooklyn, New York. Studied 1970 at Skowhegan School of Painting and Sculpture, Maine, and received M.F.A. 1971 from Brooklyn College, City University of New York. Has been included in numerous group exhibitions and has had one-man exhibitions at the Museums at Sunrise, Charleston, West Virginia, 1979; and, as part of the "Presenting West Virginia Artists" program, at Roanoke Museum of Fine Arts, Virginia, 1980. Was artist in residence, Delaware Water Gap, New Jersey, 1972. Taught at The Metropolitan Museum of Art, New York City; Yale University, New Haven, Connecticut; Virginia Museum of Fine Arts, Richmond; and Colonial Williamsburg, Virginia. Currently devotes full time to art. Lives in Brandywine, West Virginia.

101.
Seneca Rocks (B) Rts. 28, 33   1979
oil on panel
6 × 8 (15.2 × 20.3)

102.
Hevener's Cemetery   1979
oil on panel
10 × 20 (25.4 × 51)
Lent by Museums at Sunrise, Charleston,
West Virginia

Helen Johnston Vaughn

Born in Birmingham, Alabama, 1940. Received B.A. 1963 from University of Alabama at Tuscaloosa. Also studied 1959–62 at Samford University, Birmingham, Alabama; and 1973–75 at University of Alabama, Huntsville. Received Merit Award, "Alabama Art League Juried Exhibition," 1980, and Merit Award in Painting, "Exhibition South, '79," Tennessee Valley Art Center, Tuscumbia, Alabama, 1979. Was artist in residence, National Task Force for Women, Episcopal Church in America, Cleveland, Ohio, 1979. Has participated in numerous group exhibitions, including "Contemporary Painting in Alabama," Huntsville Museum of Art, Alabama, 1980. Lives in Huntsville.

I was born in Birmingham and have always lived in the South. For the past fifteen years, Huntsville, Alabama, which is located in the foothills of the Appalachian Mountains, has been my home.

It is difficult for me to determine what influence this has had on my work. An important influence, I think, has been the fact that because I am a woman who was reared in the South, home, family, friends, and the physical environment continually find their way into my work. My roots are here. I find the themes for my work here. I feel especially sensitive to my surroundings; there is a personal connection with nearly every image I paint. This probably has less to do with living in a certain area of the country than it does with the fact that I am a woman, middle-aged, who began making art at home "at the kitchen table and behind the stove." I began by painting my immediate surroundings, my family and friends; this subject matter has not changed.

left panel

124

My feeling of connectedness, of physical closeness to the people and things I paint does, I suspect, have something to do with living in Appalachia. We in the South seem to have intense feelings about things, as symbols of relationships. Life in the South is very personal; personal at a historical level. And in this area of the country, it's true, I think, that the past infuses the present.

103.
Girl on an Oriental Rug 1980
oil on linen
diptych: left panel 36 × 36 (91.4 × 91.4)
       right panel 36 × 48 (91.4 × 121.9)

right panel

Betty G. Warner

Born in Charleston, West Virginia, 1921. Received B.A. 1943 from Morris Harvey College, Charleston, West Virginia. Taught 1975–78 at Charleston Art Gallery, West Virginia. Has had numerous one-woman and group exhibitions at, among others, Salamagundi Club, New York City, 1979; West Virginia Allied Artists Annual; and Washington Arts Club, Washington, D.C., 1980. Numerous awards include Outstanding Artist of the Year, "Annual Rhododendron State Outdoor Art and Crafts Festival," Charleston, West Virginia, 1976. Is represented in numerous private and public collections. Since 1980 has taught at County Adult Education Center, Charleston.

104.
Amish Farmstead, Sundown   1979
figure 4
watercolor on paper
20 × 38 (51 × 96.5)
Lent by Dr. and Mrs. Willis Trammell, Charleston, West Virginia

I *grew up on a hill overlooking my town. From my house, I could see the valley and its surrounding hills. In summer, my playground was the higher hills beyond my house where paths known only to children led through pine thickets, past small caves, and around the steep side of the hill to Face Rock, from which we could see almost the whole world. Or we could go down the ravine to the spring where, surrounded only by woods, we could be the first Appalachian pioneers choosing a campsite.*

Inevitably, all this is a part of what I am and what my art is. My art is affected by the many ways of seeing: of looking up through the tree tops at the mountain, of looking down at the valley floor from some exhilarating summit. The constantly changing viewpoint of the hill dweller has, I believe, led me to expect visual surprises, thus to be always on the lookout for them. I find these pleasures (or they find me) in so many forms—a cattle-watering trough reflecting the August skies, one last fern sheltered by rocks against the coming winter, the geometry of a cluster of farm buildings, the calligraphy of a sassafras grove at the edge of a meadow.

My way of thinking, seeing, and painting is affected by these hills and mountains, farms and forests, snowstorms and summer showers. In these, I find visual joys that demand to be painted.

Andrew Mitchell Willis

Born in Erie, Pennsylvania, 1948. Studied 1967–69 at Columbus College of Art and Design, Ohio. Painted mural for Smithsonian Institution's summer Folklife Festival, 1978. Has been included in numerous exhibitions throughout nation, including "West Virginia Juried Exhibition," 1979, Richard J. Daley Center, Chicago, Illinois, 1978; and Vassar College Art Gallery, Poughkeepsie, New York, 1979. Cofounder with David "Blue" Lamm of Miners Art Group. Since 1979 has taught drawing and painting to senior citizens, Kanawha Valley, West Virginia.

105.
Morning at the Portal   1976
oil on canvas
22 × 39¼ (55.9 × 99.7)
Lent by Barry Spilberg, Chicago, Illinois

Living in Appalachia has had an ever-deepening effect on my art.

On arrival in West Virginia I had hoped to get work as a miner. When a back injury caused me to give up that idea, I decided to devote myself to art.

What I observed in traveling the state was neither an idealized "almost heaven" nor a stereotypical "hillbilly" scene. I saw first a sturdy people drawn from every nationality with living roots in their older generations. I saw a beautiful land whose bowels had been steadily removed in the form of coal, often with ugly results. But it was the coal miners and their families that held and continue to hold my interest and hope.

The majority of my art could be classed, I suppose, with social realism, a category that is not in particular fashion, but is as viable and strong a branch of art as any. My art is intended to reflect the concerns, anger, and aspirations of the coal fields, and to be judged by the people I presume to represent through my work.

I have had the satisfaction of approval, at times, from both old and young residents of West Virginia who cannot forgive or forget the dramas of organizing a union, recovering from the Buffalo Creek flood, or the scars of child labor.

I am striving to make my source (the struggle of life in the coal fields) and my expression in paint as one.

Ours is a story worth telling and the hope of peace unfulfilled. But I believe as Mother Jones said, "There will be no peace in the coal fields till there is justice in the coal fields."